HOW TO
START A
BUSINESS
IN THE
STATE OF
NEW JERSEY

HOW TO
START A
BUSINESS
IN THE
STATE OF
NEW JERSEY

BY LAWRENCE NOVICK

**Professor of Small Business Management & Former Director
of The Small Business Development Center at
Brookdale Community College**

Revised Edition
Copyright © 2007 by Lawrence Novick

Published by Novick Publishing, LLC
P.O. Box 725, Holmdel, New Jersey 07733
www/njbizbook.com
ISBN: 0-9614235-6-0

ABOUT THE AUTHOR

Lawrence Novick is a Management Professor at Brookdale Community College, where he instructs students on the basics of entering their own business. He established the first Small Business Management course and the Small Business Management degree option at the College. Mr. Novick is also the managing partner in an accounting firm that specializes in working with the small business owner.

Professor Novick is the former director of Brookdale's Small Business Development Center where he worked with hundreds of business people, handling any number of business-related problems. The Small Business Administration-sponsored Small Business Institute was also his responsibility, wherein students went out into the business community to assist the business person. Professor Novick has been a guest lecturer throughout the State, speaking to groups on the successful way to start and operate a small business.

This handbook is the result of his many years of teaching the subject of small business, directing government-sponsored assistance programs, and his thirty years as an accountant, working with the small business community.

PREFACE

Over the years many lengthy books have been published discussing the perils of business ownership and how people fail. Several hundred authors have printed texts that suggest how you can replace your accountant and attorney in the early years of a business. There are also a number of excellent small business management publications containing thousands of pages of material far too complicated for the new business owner.

After many years of teaching aspiring business owners and helping my own clients, I have found that there was a great demand for a text such as this one. Why not have one manual that would provide the owner with a simple means to his end wish — that being entering his own business. The materials contained within these pages do just that. The information is designed for the New Jersey business person and it covers such areas as registering your trade name, incorporation materials, working with the New Jersey sales tax bureau, free assistance agencies, and much more information about the State you intend to operate in.

It has always been my feeling that the more informed you appear to your professional the greater respect and attention you will command. Go to their office with more than just an idea; have a basic knowledge of what you intend to accomplish. I am not interested in replacing your accountant or attorney, nor teaching you the finer points of business law, or even preparing you for an intensive tax audit. Rather, I would like to help you enter the business environment just as you might prepare for a new job. Learn as much as you can, be fully aware of the pitfalls, and only then, take the final step.

If you picked up this book, you are seriously considering your own business venture and do not need to be told how to determine if you have the proper personality to be an owner. My plan is encouragement, not discouragement. I am only interested in you being fully prepared for success, not failure.

CONTENTS

1
DETERMINING
HOW MUCH
MONEY YOU NEED

Before you even think about beginning a new business you must determine how much money will be needed. It is very important to have this information at your fingertips, because one of the major reasons for small business failure is not enough beginning funds.

If you are starting your business out of a home or apartment, the operating expenses will be kept to a minimum. Most of the money you take in will end up as profit, even after paying the costs to keep your business going. By the way, be sure to check with your local town ordinances and zoning laws before you invest large sums of money in renovations or advertising. You might be surprised to discover that one of your neighbors does not want you to be in business next door to him.

When considering a new business (versus an ongoing concern) you have to be a lot more careful in the computation of the dollars necessary to get the new venture started and operating profitably. There are two very important areas which need your close attention. They are:

1. Compute how much money you will need to open up the store or business. In other words, what will it cost you before you do one dollar in sales?

2. The next area of concern is to set up some projection of how many dollars must be generated to break even, and possibly to earn enough money to also pay your personal living expenses.

Let's review and concentrate on the first section: that being the opening costs. Remember, these are probably one-time outlays of dollars that must be paid for during the first months before or shortly after the opening day. Do not simply prepare a list off the "top of your head." Write down the expenditures and obtain the most accurate costs. On the following page is a suggested list of pre-opening costs for almost any new business.

1

List of Pre-Opening Costs

1. Inventory (stock to sell in the store) $ _____

2. First month's rent   _____

3. Rent security (usually 2 or 3 months)   _____

4. Insurance (paid in advance)   _____

5. Advertising   _____

6. Deposit on utilities   _____

7. Phone installation and required deposit   _____

8. Legal and accounting fees   _____

9. Sales supplies (cards, bags, boxes)   _____

10. Improvements to the shop (decorating/
    remodeling   _____

11. Purchase of a van or truck   _____

12. Equipment and fixtures   _____

13. Registering the trade name   _____

14. License and permits   _____

15. Incorporating costs (if you select this form) _____

16. Alarm system or security gate   _____

17. Sign on the outside   _____

18. Sign on the inside   _____

19. Painting sign on a van or truck   _____

                                    TOTAL $_____

Here are some helpful hints relating to the items shown on the pre-opening cost list.

1. **Inventory**

   Most companies will require you to pay for the first order of goods C.O.D. (cash on delivery) or in advance. If any wholesaler will give you time to pay, take advantage of it. This is really an interest-free, short-term loan.

2.3. **Rent**

   This information can be obtained from the landlord when negotiating the lease. Be sure to have your lawyer review your lease before you sign it. There is no such thing as a "standard" lease.

4. **Insurance**

   Obtain the quote from your insurance agent for workmen's compensation, liability, fire, theft, and multi-peril. For additional information call the N.J. Department of Insurance at (609) 292-2516. Be sure to get workers compensation insurance to cover any employees.

5. **Advertising**

   This is a tough area. This amount will vary greatly depending on the media you use. Make sure you get written quotes for your ads.

6.7. **Utilities**

   The electric, gas, and phone companies can provide exact amounts for these categories.

8. **Legal and accounting fees**

   Ask your professional for a realistic estimated cost of services to be rendered.

9. **Sales supplies**

   This section takes in all size bags, business cards, stationery and sales invoices.

10. **Improvements**

   This is another large expenditure, so be careful. This area includes walls (paneling), pegboard, drop ceilings, lights, bathrooms, shelving, cabinets, display fixtures, mirrors, etc. Sometimes the landlord may be willing to do some or all of the improvements in return for an increase in the monthly rent.

11. **Vehicle**

   Purchase only if you need one.

12. **Equipment and fixtures**
    In this area be sure to include cash registers, adding machines, file cabinets, safe, desk, chairs, tables, etc.

13. **Registering trade name**
    Completed at your County Clerk's office — about $55.00.

14. **Licenses and Permits**
    Contact the N.J. State Dept. of Licenses and Permits, Dept. of State, State House, CN 300, Trenton, N.J. 08625-0300 – Attn.: Ombudsman (609) 777-0885.

15. **Incorporation**
    Let your attorney inform you of the amount of money required here (or you may file on your own).

16-19. **Security systems, signs**
    Get at least three separate quotes for each of these items. Remember, you need a sign big enough for people to see.

Now that you have figured out how much money you need to start the business, go ahead and count what you have on hand and how much you will be able to borrow. If you cannot come up with the amount necessary to get your business started, give it a hard close second look. Then go back and reevaluate the pre-opening list and costs. Also, don't forget, you may need money in the first six months to carry you through any initial slow period.

2
COMPUTING A
BREAKEVEN TO OPERATE
THE BUSINESS

We are now ready to review the second area, which concerns itself with figuring out a breakeven point. It will be difficult to stay in business if you cannot turn a profit. This part of the book will show you how to set up a budget of income and expenses. Under most conditions the statement of income and expenses starts with receipts (sales, fees, commissions, etc.) on the top and lists all the expenses thereafter. The total expenses are deducted from sales to reach a profit or loss, such as:

AL'S PHOTO SHOP
Month of November

Sale of photos		$1200
Expenses		
Supplies	500	
Phone	45	
Rent	230	
Auto expenses	110	
Total expenses		885
NET PROFIT		**$315**

In working out the breakeven, the first step is to set down what you feel will be the costs to operate the business. Let's also make an assumption that your present job pays you $1,000.00 per month gross pay before tax deductions, and that you need to make at least this same amount if you go out on your own.

Here comes the tough part. You must try to estimate the monthly operating costs as accurately as possible. The expenses might include the following items and here we will use estimated amounts to show how to set up the schedule.

	Monthly Estimated Costs
Expenses — Itemized	
Rent	$ 500
Help	400
Utilities	150
Advertising	150
Telephone	80
Delivery Costs	50
Insurance	50
Sales Supplies	40
Water	15
TOTAL	$1435
Total expenses	$1435
Your present earnings	1000
SALES	$2435

Monthly	$2435
Less Expenses to Operate	1435
Net Profit	$1000

```
              Projected Statement of Income & Expenses
  Sales                                              $4,870
  Cost of sales 50%                                  -2,435
                                  Gross Profit        $2,435
  Expenses
      Rent              $ 500
      Help                400
      Utilities           150
      Advertising         150
      Telephone            80
      Delivery Costs       50
      Insurance            50
      Sales Supplies       40
      Water                15
                                  Total expenses      1,435
                                  Net Profit         $1,000
```

This statement shows that you will have to generate net sales or a gross profit of $2,435.00 in order to pay all your expenses and provide a salary to you of $1,000 per month. In income statement form the breakeven computation might appear as follows:

Be careful. If there are any monthly notes or loans to be paid, these should be included in your estimate of expenses for a total monthly cash outlay.

The projected income statement for a retail business is set up a little different. A brief accounting lesson for retail sales: If your selling price is double the cost of your goods, you make a 50% gross profit. To generate $2,435.00 gross profit you must have sales of $4,870.00 and the statement will look like the following (this is also a way to check your computation):

Be sure to try and obtain accurate costs. The problem here is that you are estimating sales of $4,870 and if the business cannot

3
OBTAINING
THE CAPITAL
TO START

Let's begin to look at where and how you can get the money. Most inexperienced business people immediately think of their bank or some government agency to come up with the bulk of the funds. There are many sources of money for the new business that should be pursued. Once again, before committing yourself to a lease, leaving your full time job or signing a long-term contract, make sure you have your financing in order. The biggest problem of most new owners is that they do not start with enough money in the early years or are incapable of acquiring extra needed dollars later on. Don't get caught up in this trap. Do your planning before you start or — don't start.

The problem here is not whether to borrow, how much interest you should be paying, or how long the payout should be. If you really want to begin your business, where or how you obtain your money or capital will not matter.

Your starting funds may come from one or more of the following sources:

- **Personal funds** — savings account, etc.
- **Personal Bank Loan** — signature or collateral
- **Trade Credit** — here you purchase inventory and pay in 30 to 90 days
- **Loan from a vendor or supplier** — at times vending companies may pay your commissions in advance
- **Friends** — be prepared to pay interest on the loan
- **Small Loan Companies** — very high interest rate
- **Credit Unions**
- **Loans on your Life Insurance** — this is usually very low interest

- **Advance Borrowing through a Credit Card** — very high interest
- **Overdraft Checking Account Loans**
- **Small Business Administration**
- **Second Mortgage on your home**
- **Refinancing a first mortgage on your home**
- **Loans from pension funds**
- **Equipment loans or leases** — in these situations the seller of the equipment may allow you to pay for the item over a fixed period of time
- **N. J. Economic Development Authority**

One important factor to consider when you borrow money is to make sure you add the monthly payments into your budget of cash flow along with your expenses.

Another point to incorporate into your business thinking is to *be sure to pay all your notes on time.* Your credit rating with lenders is your most important asset. Without the ability to borrow, you may not be able to expand to other areas, increase your inventory, or even take on more help. Once you neglect to make timely payments on your loans, you effectively cut off your line of credit. When you borrow, do so wisely, and *always* pay your monthly obligation.

A small clue about our banking institutions. At times one gets the feeling they like to lend their money to people who don't need it. When you go to your bank, *look good*, and if they are willing to make a loan, borrow a little more than you need. If you go back a year later when business is slow, you may not be able to get the additional monies.

Before going to any bank to borrow money, find out the bank's policies by contacting lending institutions, and ask the following:

— **Are they lending to borrowers such as yourself**

— **What is the present interest rate — remember the rate may vary with different types of loans**

— **What information will they want to review**

Here is a method that has been used effectively when attempting to get loan approval for a new business. Be prepared and have all your papers in order when you go to the bank.

FOR AN EXISTING OR NEW BUSINESS

— Know exactly how much you need
— Be able to tell the loan officer how the money will help you, such as:
  — increase sales
  — purchase equipment
  — expand your shop
  — hire new employees
  — increase inventory
  — pay for a new advertising program
  — etc.
— Show the officer how these new funds will make you more money
— Have a payment plan in mind (how long before the bank will get its money back)

FOR A NEW BUSINESS

— Describe in detail the type of business to be established
— Be sure to explain your experience and management capabilities related to the business
— Bring along a brief history of yourself and why you are going into this particular business
— Show how much money you or others will invest in the business
— Have with you a current balance sheet listing all personal assets and liabilities
— Prepare a detailed projection of earnings for the first year the business will operate
— If you are incorporated, be aware that the bank may still want you to sign personally on the loan

I enjoy relating a story of how I got my first business loan. A client friend of mine was going to introduce me to his banker from whom I hoped to borrow $5,000 for one year. My preparation for the meeting included a financial history of my firm, a personal resume, why I needed the money, and when I would repay the loan. When I met my friend and discussed the loan, we agreed that a request of $10,000 would no doubt at least get me $5,000. In the elevator going down to the banker I decided to ask for $15,000 and negotiate down to $5,000 or $10,000. After having met the loan officer and having spoken to him for several minutes, I felt more confident and my reply to his question of "How Much?" was $20,000. Much to my surprise, he said, "OK, how long before you can repay it?" I was delighted in having obtained four times what I needed. I took the $20,000, put $15,000 in a savings account and utilized the $5,000 in the business. After two months I repaid $5,000 on the loan and three months later sent the lender another $7,000. The bank thought I was great. Here I had paid back 60% of the loan in the first five months! In doing so I had earned interest on the extra money borrowed and also saved interest expense by repaying the loan early. My credit record was established and by the end of the twelve months the entire loan was paid off.

4
YOUR BOOKKEEPING SYSTEM

Thus far we have concerned ourselves with determining your financial needs and how to fill them. Now let's proceed to the next step, setting up a bookkeeping system. Once you make the decision to go into your own business, you will be expending funds. The simplest way to keep track of your expenses will be through the use of a checkbook.

If at any time you want to prove that your expenses are business-related and deductible, this is much easier to do if the costs are paid for by a business check. Do not begin paying your bills by cash or even with a small pocket-size checkbook. Also, try not to pay business expenses from your personal checkbook. Remember, attempt to look like a legitimate business concern to all parties concerned about your operation; open a business checking account, and save all your bills.

There are minimum records that must be kept for yourself, the business, and your accountant. Whether you operate by check or cash, you must be able to compute a profit or loss so a tax return can be completed. The outline on page 14 shows the minimum records to maintain for your business.

Here is some sound advice on your record-keeping system and books of original entry.

1. Save all bills and invoices; mark them when paid, noting whether check or cash, and the date paid. After the invoice is paid, be sure to file it where you can locate the bill if needed again.

STATEMENT No. *1612C*

TO *JAMY'S* _____20___

TERMS:

500 LBS.		#2 FLOUR		$	25	00
		Paid				
		Ch. # 162				
		5-23-2				

A PAID INVOICE

13

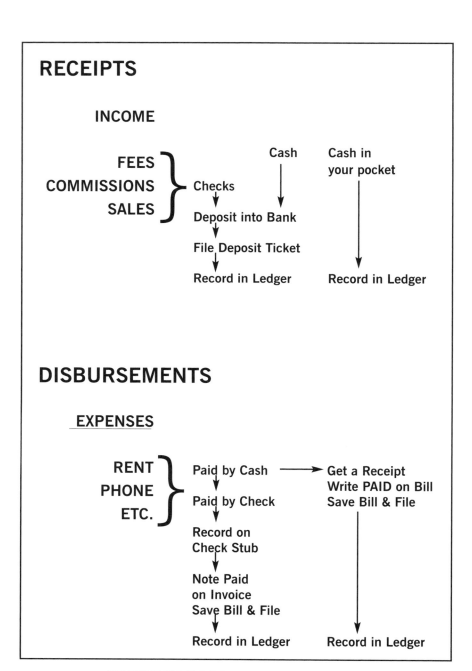

RECEIPTS

INCOME

FEES
COMMISSIONS
SALES

Checks

Cash

Cash in
your pocket

Deposit into Bank

File Deposit Ticket

Record in Ledger

Record in Ledger

DISBURSEMENTS

EXPENSES

RENT
PHONE
ETC.

Paid by Cash ⟶ Get a Receipt
Write PAID on Bill
Paid by Check   Save Bill & File

Record on
Check Stub

Note Paid
on Invoice
Save Bill & File

Record in Ledger

Record in Ledger

MINIMUM RECORDS TO MAINTAIN

2. Keep a record of all the miles put on your vehicle. Before anything happens, you will have visited an attorney, looked at stores, gone to suppliers and made calls on builders. All these trips are legitimate deductions, even if you are unable to start the business.

NOVEMBER 20____

9	MONDAY

To Red Bank
18 miles
Look at store

10	TUESDAY

11	WEDNESDAY

Visit Donut Shoppe
Lakewood
36 miles
Parking 25¢

NOVEMBER 20____

THURSDAY	12

FRIDAY	13

went to Rex Lyon
Attorney, East
Hanover
72 miles

SATURDAY	14

bought Journal
Cash $5.95   8 miles

SUNDAY	15

DIARY

3. **Open and start using a business-type checking account, with your name imprinted on the checks. If you registered the trade name, this should also appear on your checks.**

When getting your first business checking account, I would recommend the commercial type setup with a larger size check and checkstub. The best type would be the one that uses a three-ring binder that looks like this.

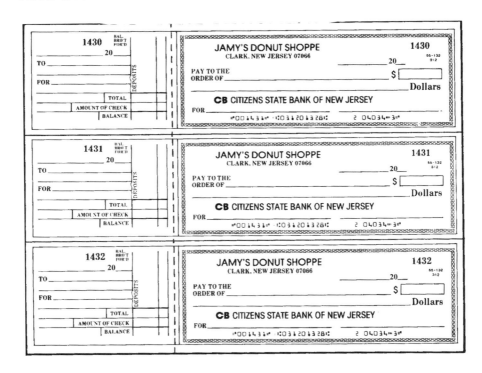

BUSINESS SIZE CHECKS AND
CHECK STUBS

The stub allows enough space to fully explain what is written on the check. The stub can be removed easily from the notebook so that a bookkeeper or accountant can copy information from the stub and into a journal to summarize the checks written. When the task is completed, the stubs can be returned to the notebook and placed back into numerical order.

Many people make the mistake of starting with the small pocket size type. This tiny checkbook is too small to provide adequate information on the check or stub as can be seen from the illustration.

DATE	#		PAYEE	DEBIT	CREDIT	BAL.

JAMY'S DONUT SHOPPE
CLARK, NEW JERSEY 07066   143

                                                                        65-132
                                                                        312
                                                        _____20___

PAY TO THE
ORDER OF _____ $ [_____]

_____ Dollars

CB CITIZENS STATE BANK OF NEW JERSEY

FOR _____

⑈00 ⅃⅃431⑈ ⅃:03 ⅃20 ⅃3 28⑈   2 0⅃034⑈3⑈

**POCKET SIZE
CHECKBOOK**

ONE-WRITE SYSTEM

I will explain this system to you, but suggest some caution in starting out with this setup. More than likely, your funds will be limited in the beginning, so you might want to watch your expenditures. A one-write check system could cost you anywhere from $55 to $200 to start. Wait a reasonable length of time to see how business will be, for you can change to this system of bookkeeping at any time.

One of the most important bookkeeping functions is to prepare a summary of all the checks written in your checkbook. The book setup to summarize these checks is called a disbursements journal. When using a regular checking account, your write-up of a check disbursements journal would be completed as follows:

1. **You write the check for rent — $375.00**

2. **Then you enter this information on the stub**

3. **From the stub you would prepare a check disbursements journal like the one shown below.**

DATE	PAYEE	CH. #	AMOUNT	RENT	PURCHASES	PHONE	GEN. ITEMS
5/5	Landlord	106	375.	375.			

CHECK DISBURSEMENTS JOURNAL

When using a one-write type of system, you would only have to do one writing. Actually, the system is rather simple for it uses a carbon strip on the back of the check.

When you write the check, you prepare the check stub and disbursements journal at the same time. This type of bookkeeping system is a great time saver, avoids errors, and is even more effective for payroll record keeping. A typical one-write system for writing checks is shown below.

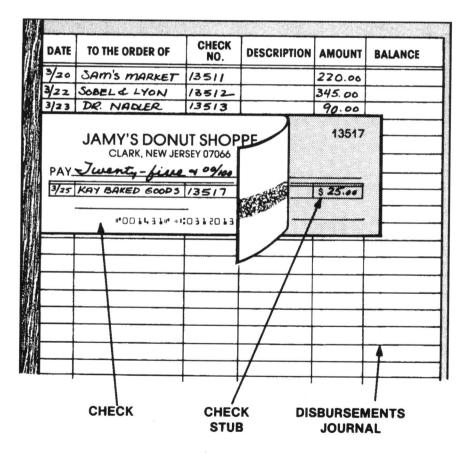

DATE	TO THE ORDER OF	CHECK NO.	DESCRIPTION	AMOUNT	BALANCE
3/20	SAM's MARKET	13511		220.00	
3/22	SOBEL & LYON	13512		345.00	
3/23	DR. NADLER	13513		90.00	
3/25	KAY BAKED GOODS	13517		$25.00	

JAMY'S DONUT SHOPPE
CLARK, NEW JERSEY 07066
PAY Twenty-five & 00/100

13517

"00143" "03120 13"

CHECK   CHECK STUB   DISBURSEMENTS JOURNAL

**ONE-WRITE SYSTEM
DISBURSEMENTS JOURNAL**

By using a payroll one-write system you can produce the check, your checkstub, the employee's paystub, payroll journal, and employee's earnings card with one entry. An illustration is shown below.

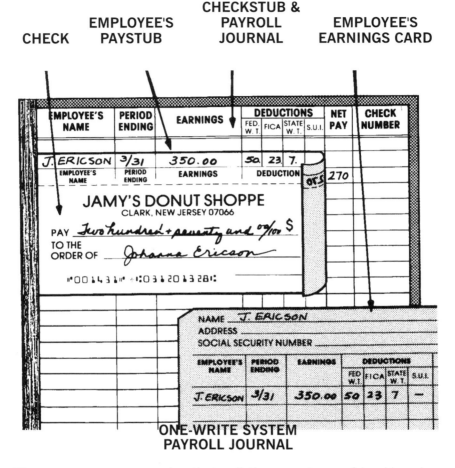

CHECK **EMPLOYEE'S PAYSTUB** **CHECKSTUB & PAYROLL JOURNAL** **EMPLOYEE'S EARNINGS CARD**

ONE-WRITE SYSTEM
PAYROLL JOURNAL

There are many companies that sell these systems of bookkeeping. Have them come speak to you and give you the information and costs for the setup. Before making a final decision, be sure to check with your accountant.

Remember the clearer your records, the easier it will be for your financial advisor to prepare financial statements and do your tax returns.

5
REGISTERING
YOUR
TRADE NAME

When starting a business, many people like to select a name that is different from their own. Often they wish to use a name or phrase that is "catchy" or describes their shop. This name, which is different from their own, is known as a trade name.

The major reason for filing a trade name certificate is to make certain that you can prevent someone else from using your name. You would be very upset if another new business opened in the general area as yours and used the same trade name. After you spend a lot of money advertising Jamy's Donut Shoppe, you do not want to see someone else open up with the same name over the door. Once you file "Jamy's Donut Shoppe," you will have a better chance of preventing other people from using the same trade name in your county.

If you do not incorporate your business, you should help protect your trade name by filing a Trade Name Certificate within the county that you locate your company. The bank will also want to see your approved trade name certificate before allowing you to open a checking account under this fictitious name.

A sample trade name certificate form is shown on the next page for your review. This sheet must be completed, notarized, and then four copies brought to the courthouse in the county you locate the business. The cost will be about $50.00 for the filing.

For informational purposes there are two abbreviations used in trade name presentations.

T/A means "trading as"

and

D.B.A. means "doing business as"

As an example, Jon and Amy Carlin open the donut business and name it Jamy's Donut Shoppe. They may show their name on business checks as:

Jon and Amy Carlin T/A
Jamy's Donut Shoppe

or

Jon and Amy Carlin D.B.A.
Jamy's Donut Shoppe

PLEASE NOTE THAT INFORMATION BECOMES PUBLIC RECORD
CERTIFICATE OF TRADE NAME
Monmouth County, New Jersey
M. CLAIRE FRENCH, COUNTY CLERK   732-431-7324

The undersigned hereby certifies the following:

1. The name under which the undersigned is about to transact business
2. The location where the said business will be conducted
3. The type of business to be conducted by the undersigned
4. The full name(s) and address of each person(s) connected with the said business as owner(s)
5. The subscriber(s), who, if non-resident(s) of the State of New Jersey, do hereby appoint and constitute the County Clerk of the County wherein this Certificate shall be filed our true and lawful attorney, upon whom all original process in any action or legal proceeding against said firm or partnership may be served, and hereby agree that such original process which may be served on such County Clerk shall be of the same force and validity as if served upon said non-resident partner or partners, and the authority hereby granted shall continue in force so long as the firm or partnership does business in the State of New Jersey under said name.

TRADE NAME OR DBA _____

CORPORATION NAME _____

ADDRESS 1 _____

ADDRESS 2 _____

CITY/STATE/ZIP _____

PHONE NUMBER (OPTIONAL)_____

DATE REGISTERED _____

DESCRIPTION OF BUSINESS _____

OWNER #1 NAME_____

STREET ADDRESS_____

CITY/STATE/ZIP_____

SIGNATURE_____

OWNER #2 NAME_____

STREET ADDRESS_____

CITY/STATE/ZIP_____

SIGNATURE_____

OWNER #3 NAME_____

STREET ADDRESS_____

CITY/STATE/ZIP_____

SIGNATURE_____

OWNER #4 NAME_____

STREET ADDRESS_____

CITY/STATE/ZIP_____

SIGNATURE_____

State of New Jersey
County of Monmouth

Sworn and subscribed to before me this _____ day of _____, 20____

_____
Notary Public

The locations of the County Court Houses in the State of New Jersey are noted on the following pages. Be sure to call the county clerk before bringing your form there. On the next page is a copy of the instruction sheet given to trade name applicants in Monmouth County.

LOCATIONS OF THE
NEW JERSEY COUNTY CLERKS

ATLANTIC COUNTY
County Clerk: Michael J. Garvin
5901 Main Street, Box 2005
Mays Landing, NJ 08330
(609) 641-7867
Record Room: (609) 645-5842
Fax: (609) 625-4738

BERGEN COUNTY
County Clerk: Kathleen A. Donovan
One Bergen Plaza, Room 122
Hackensack, NJ 07601-7000
(201) 336-7020
Fax (201-336-7002
Registry Division, Room 214
(201) 646-2082

BURLINGTON COUNTY
County Clerk: Philiip E. Haines
Court Complex, 1st Floor
49 Rancocas Road
Mount Holly, NJ 08060
(609) 265-5189
Fax: (609) 265-0696

CAMDEN COUNTY
County Clerk: James Beach
6th Street Entrance, Suite 316
PO Box 150
Camden, NJ 08101-0150
(865) 225-7219
Fax (856)-756-2213

CAPE MAY COUNTY
County Clerk: Angela F. Pulvino
7 N. Main St., PO Box 5000
Cape May, NJ 08210-5000
(609) 465-1013
Fax: (609) 465-8625

CUMBERLAND COUNTY
County Clerk: Gloria Noto
Court House Bldg.
PO Box 716, 60 West Broad St.
Bridgeton, NJ 08302
(856) 451-8000, Ext. 221
Fax: (856) 455-1410

ESSEX COUNTY
County Clerk: Patrick J. McNally
247 Hall of Records
469 Dr. Martin Luther King Blvd.
Newark, NJ 07102
(973) 621-4921
Fax: (973) 621-2527/2537

GLOUCESTER COUNTY
County Clerk: James N. Hogan
Court House, 1st Floor
1 N. Broad St., PO Box 129
Woodbury, NJ 08096-3327
(856) 853-3241, 853-3230
Fax: (856) 853-3327

HUDSON COUNTY
County Clerk: Janet E. Haynes
Brennan Courthouse
584 Newark Ave.
Jersey City, NJ 07306
(201) 795-6112
Fax: (201) 795-2581

HUNTERDON COUNTY
County Clerk: Dorothy K. Tirpok
Hall of Records
71 Main Street
Flemington, NJ 08822
(908) 788-1214
Fax: (908)782-4068

PROCEDURE FOR FILING A TRADE NAME
IN MONMOUTH COUNTY

1. Search the records in the Deed Room of the County Clerk's Office in Freehold for the availability of the name you wish to file. This will require searching in the computer and in the books.

2. Be aware that filing a trade name is only effective in the county in which you file; it is possible that the business name exists in another county.

3. The Certificate of Trade Name must be filled out and notarized in our office. **DO NOT SIGN THE FORM UNTIL YOU ARE IN THE RECORDING OFFICE.** The following will be required:

    a. Identification (driver's license, passport, etc.)
    b. $54.00 cash or money order to record
    c. All parties involved must be present

4. We will keep the original, send a copy to the Secretary of State and send you two copies within seven days from the day it is dropped off for recording, one of which you will give to your bank to open a business account.

5. You must also register your business with the State of New Jersey, Division of Taxation in Trenton (New Business Guide and Information provided when you bring the Trade Name Form in for recording).

MONMOUTH COUNTY CHECKLIST FOR
REGISTERING A TRADE NAME

MERCER COUNTY

County Clerk: Catherine DiCostanzo
100 Court House Annex
209 S. Broad Street, PO Box 8068
Trenton, NJ 08650-0068
(609) 989-6494
Fax: (609) 989-1111

MIDDLESEX COUNTY

County Clerk: Elaine Flynn
75 Bayard Street, 4th Floor
PO Box 1110
New Brunswick, NJ 08901-1110
(732) 745-3827
Fax: (732) 745-2170

MONMOUTH COUNTY

County Clerk: M. Claire French
300 Halls Mill Road
Freehold, NJ 07728-1254
(732) 431-7324
Fax: (732) 409-7566

MORRIS COUNTY

County Clerk: Jan Bramball
Administrative & Records Bldg.
PO Box 315 - Court Street
Morristown, NJ 07963-0315
(973) 285-6066
Fax: (973) 285-5233

OCEAN COUNTY

County Clerk: M. Dean Haines
105 Court House
118 Washington St.
PO Box 2191
Toms River, NJ 08754
(732) 929-2018 or 2118
Fax: (732) 349-4336

PASSAIC COUNTY

County Clerk: Ronni Nochimson
401 Grand St., Room 130
Paterson, NJ 07505
(973) 225-3632
Fax: (973) 754-1920

SALEM COUNTY

County Clerk: Gilda T. Gill
92 Market Street, PO Box 18
Salem, NJ 08079
(856) 935-7510, Ext. 8208
Fax: (856) 935-8882

SOMERSET COUNTY

County Clerk: Brett Radi
Adm. Bldg., Room 110
PO Box 3000, 20 Grove Street
Somerville, NJ 08876-1262
(908) 231-7013
Fax: (908) 253-8853

SUSSEX COUNTY

County Clerk: Erma Gormley
Hall of Records Bldg.
4 Park Place
Newton, NJ 07860-1795
(973) 579-0900
Fax: (973) 383-7493

UNION COUNTY

County Clerk: Joanne Rajoppi
105 Court House, 1st Flr.
2 Broad St., PO Box 6073
Elizabeth, NJ 07207
(908) 527-4998 or 99
Fax: (908) 558-2589

WARREN COUNTY

County Clerk: Terrance D. Lee
413 2nd Street
Belvidere, NJ 07823-1500
(908) 475-6214
Fax: (908) 475-6208

6
OBTAINING A FEDERAL EMPLOYMENT NUMBER AND REGISTERING WITH THE STATE OF NEW JERSEY

When you go to the bank to start a business checking account, they will require a federal identification number. This particular number is obtained through application to the Internal Revenue Service on Form SS4. The nine-digit number that will be assigned to your company is like a social security number for a business.

Regardless of the type of ownership you select, the bank will want to see your identification number. If you choose the partnership or corporate organization in which to operate, the federal government requires that you have a federal identification number.

The federal SS4 form is usually one of the major papers completed by your accountant when he "sets up your books." The application is relatively simple to complete and can be done by following the step-by-step directions on the form. The completed form is shown on page 27 with explanations where necessary. After you complete the application, sign on the bottom and mail to the I.R.S., 1040 Waverly Avenue, Holtsville, New York 00501. Remember, this is a federal form and has nothing to do with the State of New Jersey.

INSTRUCTIONS TO COMPLETE THE FORM
(Key to form numbers)

1. Use your full name; if partnership or corporation, place that name on this line.

2. Enter your trade name.

3–7. Self-explanatory.

8a. Check only one box; if sole proprietor, fill in your Social Security number.

9. Usually "Started a New Business" will be checked.

Form **SS-4**	**Application for Employer Identification Number**	OMB No. 1545-0003

Form **SS-4**
(Rev. February 2006)
Department of the Treasury
Internal Revenue Service

Application for Employer Identification Number
(For use by employers, corporations, partnerships, trusts, estates, churches, government agencies, Indian tribal entities, certain individuals, and others.)
► See separate instructions for each line. ► Keep a copy for your records.

OMB No. 1545-0003

EIN

Type or print clearly.

1 Legal name of entity (or individual) for whom the EIN is being requested
THE CARLIN PARTNERSHIP

2 Trade name of business (if different from name on line 1)
JAMY'S DONUT SHOPPE

3 Executor, administrator, trustee, "care of" name

4a Mailing address (room, apt., suite no. and street, or P.O. box)
44 DONNA COURT

5a Street address (if different) (Do not enter a P.O. box.)

4b City, state, and ZIP code
CLARK, NEW JERSEY 07066

5b City, state, and ZIP code

6 County and state where principal business is located
UNION, NEW JERSEY

7a Name of principal officer, general partner, grantor, owner, or trustor
AMY CARLIN

7b SSN, ITIN, or EIN
123-45-6789

8a Type of entity (check only one box)
☐ Sole proprietor (SSN)
☑ Partnership
☐ Corporation (enter form number to be filed) ►
☐ Personal service corporation
☐ Church or church-controlled organization
☐ Other nonprofit organization (specify) ►
☐ Other (specify) ►

☐ Estate (SSN of decedent)
☐ Plan administrator (SSN)
☐ Trust (SSN of grantor)
☐ National Guard ☐ State/local government
☐ Farmers' cooperative ☐ Federal government/military
☐ REMIC ☐ Indian tribal governments/enterprises
Group Exemption Number (GEN) ►

8b If a corporation, name the state or foreign country (if applicable) where incorporated
State
Foreign country

9 Reason for applying (check only one box)
☑ Started new business (specify type) ► BAKERY
☐ Hired employees (Check the box and see line 12.)
☐ Compliance with IRS withholding regulations
☐ Other (specify) ►

☐ Banking purpose (specify purpose) ►
☐ Changed type of organization (specify new type) ►
☐ Purchased going business
☐ Created a trust (specify type) ►
☐ Created a pension plan (specify type) ►

10 Date business started or acquired (month, day, year). See instructions.
JANUARY 1, 2007

11 Closing month of accounting year
DECEMBER

12 First date wages or annuities were paid (month, day, year). **Note.** If applicant is a withholding agent, enter date income will first be paid to nonresident alien. (month, day, year) . . . . ► FEBRUARY 1, 2007

13 Highest number of employees expected in the next 12 months (enter -0- if none).

	Agricultural	Household	Other
Do you expect to have $1,000 or less in employment tax liability for the calendar year? ☑ Yes ☐ No. (If you expect to pay $4,000 or less in wages, you can mark yes.)			3

14 Check **one** box that best describes the principal activity of your business. ☐ Health care & social assistance ☐ Wholesale-agent/broker
☐ Construction ☐ Rental & leasing ☐ Transportation & warehousing ☐ Accommodation & food service ☐ Wholesale-other ☑ Retail
☐ Real estate ☐ Manufacturing ☐ Finance & insurance ☐ Other (specify)

15 Indicate principal line of merchandise sold, specific construction work done, products produced, or services provided.
BAKERY PRODUCTS

16a Has the applicant ever applied for an employer identification number for this or any other business? . . . . ☐ Yes ☑ No
Note. If "Yes," please complete lines 16b and 16c.

16b If you checked "Yes" on line 16a, give applicant's legal name and trade name shown on prior application if different from line 1 or 2 above.
Legal name ► Trade name ►

16c Approximate date when, and city and state where, the application was filed. Enter previous employer identification number if known.
Approximate date when filed (mo., day, year) City and state where filed Previous EIN

Third Party Designee	Complete this section **only** if you want to authorize the named individual to receive the entity's EIN and answer questions about the completion of this form.	
	Designee's name	Designee's telephone number (include area code) ( )
	Address and ZIP code	Designee's fax number (include area code) ( )

Under penalties of perjury, I declare that I have examined this application, and to the best of my knowledge and belief, it is true, correct, and complete.

Name and title (type or print clearly) ► AMY CARLIN, PARTNER

Applicant's telephone number (include area code)
(732) 555-2738

Signature ► Date ►

Applicant's fax number (include area code)
(732) 555-2739

For Privacy Act and Paperwork Reduction Act Notice, see separate instructions. Cat. No. 16055N Form **SS-4** (Rev. 2-2006)

APPLICATION FOR
EMPLOYER IDENTIFICATION NUMBER

Instructions for Form SS-4

(Rev. February 2006)

Department of the Treasury
Internal Revenue Service

Application for Employer Identification Number

Section references are to the Internal Revenue Code unless otherwise noted.

General Instructions

Use these instructions to complete Form SS-4, Application for Employer Identification Number. Also see *Do I Need an EIN?* on page 2 of Form SS-4.

Purpose of Form

Use Form SS-4 to apply for an employer identification number (EIN). An EIN is a nine-digit number (for example, 12-3456789) assigned to sole proprietors, corporations, partnerships, estates, trusts, and other entities for tax filing and reporting purposes. The information you provide on this form will establish your business tax account.

 An EIN is for use in connection with your business activities only. Do not use your EIN in place of your social security number (SSN).

Reminders

Apply online. Generally, you can apply for and receive an EIN online using the Internet. See *How To Apply* below.

File only one Form SS-4. Generally, a sole proprietor should file only one Form SS-4 and needs only one EIN, regardless of the number of businesses operated as a sole proprietorship or trade names under which a business operates. However, if the proprietorship incorporates or enters into a partnership, a new EIN is required. Also, each corporation in an affiliated group must have its own EIN.

EIN applied for, but not received. If you do not have an EIN by the time a return is due, write "Applied For" and the date you applied in the space shown for the number. Do not show your SSN as an EIN on returns.

If you do not have an EIN by the time a tax deposit is due, send your payment to the Internal Revenue Service Center for your filing area as shown in the instructions for the form that you are filing. Make your check or money order payable to the "United States Treasury" and show your name (as shown on Form SS-4), address, type of tax, period covered, and date you applied for an EIN.

Federal tax deposits. New employers that have a federal tax obligation will be pre-enrolled in the Electronic Federal Tax Payment System (EFTPS). EFTPS allows you to make all of your federal tax payments online at *www.eftps.gov* or by telephone. Shortly after we have assigned you your EIN, you will receive instructions by mail for activating your EFTPS enrollment. You will also receive an EFTPS Personal Identification Number (PIN) that you will use to make your payments, as well as instructions for obtaining an Internet password you will need to make payments online.

If you are not required to make deposits by EFTPS, you can use Form 8109, Federal Tax Deposit (FTD) Coupon, to make deposits at an authorized depositary. If

you would like to receive Form 8109, call 1-800-829-4933. Allow 5 to 6 weeks for delivery. For more information on federal tax deposits, see Pub. 15 (Circular E).

How To Apply

You can apply for an EIN online, by telephone, by fax, or by mail depending on how soon you need to use the EIN. Use only one method for each entity so you do not receive more than one EIN for an entity.

Online. Generally, you can receive your EIN by Internet and use it immediately to file a return or make a payment. Go to the IRS website at *www.irs.gov/businesses* and click on Employer ID Numbers.

Applicants that may not apply online. The online application process is not yet available to:
• Applicants with foreign addresses (including Puerto Rico),
• Limited Liability Companies (LLCs) that have not yet determined their entity classification for federal tax purposes (see *Limited liability company (LLC)* on page 4),
• Real Estate Investment Conduits (REMICs),
• State and local governments,
• Federal Government/Military, and
• Indian Tribal Governments/Enterprises.

Telephone. You can receive your EIN by telephone and use it immediately to file a return or make a payment. Call the IRS at 1-800-829-4933. (International applicants must call 215-516-6999.) The hours of operation are 7:00 a.m. to 10:00 p.m. local time (Pacific time for Alaska and Hawaii). The person making the call must be authorized to sign the form or be an authorized designee. See *Signature* and *Third Party Designee* on page 6. Also see the *TIP* below.

If you are applying by telephone, it will be helpful to complete Form SS-4 before contacting the IRS. An IRS representative will use the information from the Form SS-4 to establish your account and assign you an EIN. Write the number you are given on the upper right corner of the form and sign and date it. Keep this copy for your records.

If requested by an IRS representative, mail or fax (facsimile) the signed Form SS-4 (including any Third Party Designee authorization) within 24 hours to the IRS address provided by the IRS representative.

TIP *Taxpayer representatives can apply for an EIN on behalf of their client and request that the EIN be faxed to their client on the same day. Note. By using this procedure, you are authorizing the IRS to fax the EIN without a cover sheet.*

Fax. Under the Fax-TIN program, you can receive your EIN by fax within 4 business days. Complete and fax Form SS-4 to the IRS using the Fax-TIN number listed on page 2 for your state. A long-distance charge to callers outside of the local calling area will apply. Fax-TIN

Cat. No. 62736F

INSTRUCTIONS FOR APPLICATION FOR EMPLOYER IDENTIFICATION NUMBER

numbers can only be used to apply for an EIN. The numbers may change without notice. Fax-TIN is available 24 hours a day, 7 days a week.

Be sure to provide your fax number so the IRS can fax the EIN back to you.

Note. By using this procedure, you are authorizing the IRS to fax the EIN without a cover sheet.

Mail. Complete Form SS-4 at least 4 to 5 weeks before you will need an EIN. Sign and date the application and mail it to the service center address for your state. You will receive your EIN in the mail in approximately 4 weeks. See also *Third Party Designee* on page 6.

Call 1-800-829-4933 to verify a number or to ask about the status of an application by mail.

Where to Fax or File

If your principal business, office or agency, or legal residence in the case of an individual, is located in:	Fax or file with the "Internal Revenue Service Center" at:
Connecticut, Delaware, District of Columbia, Florida, Georgia, Maine, Maryland, Massachusetts, New Hampshire, New Jersey, New York, North Carolina, Ohio, Pennsylvania, Rhode Island, South Carolina, Vermont, Virginia, West Virginia	Attn: EIN Operation Holtsville, NY 11742 Fax-TIN: 631-447-8960
Illinois, Indiana, Kentucky, Michigan	Attn: EIN Operation Cincinnati, OH 45999 Fax-TIN: 859-669-5760
Alabama, Alaska, Arizona, Arkansas, California, Colorado, Hawaii, Idaho, Iowa, Kansas, Louisiana, Minnesota, Mississippi, Missouri, Montana, Nebraska, Nevada, New Mexico, North Dakota, Oklahoma, Oregon, South Dakota, Tennessee, Texas, Utah, Washington, Wisconsin, Wyoming	Attn: EIN Operation Philadelphia, PA 19255 Fax-TIN: 859-669-5760
If you have no legal residence, principal place of business, or principal office or agency in any state:	Attn: EIN Operation Philadelphia, PA 19255 Fax-TIN: 215-516-1040

How To Get Forms and Publications

Phone. Call 1-800-TAX-FORM (1-800-829-3676) to order forms, instructions, and publications. You should receive your order or notification of its status within 10 workdays.

Internet. You can access the IRS website 24 hours a day, 7 days a week at *www.irs.gov* to download forms, instructions, and publications.

CD-ROM. For small businesses, return preparers, or others who may frequently need tax forms or publications, a CD-ROM containing over 2,000 tax products (including many prior year forms) can be purchased from the National Technical Information Service (NTIS).

To order Pub. 1796, IRS Tax Products CD, call 1-877-CDFORMS (1-877-233-6767) toll free or connect to *www.irs.gov/cdorders*.

Tax Help for Your Business

IRS-sponsored Small Business Workshops provide information about your federal and state tax obligations. For information about workshops in your area, call 1-800-829-4933.

Related Forms and Publications

The following forms and instructions may be useful to filers of Form SS-4.
● Form 990-T, Exempt Organization Business Income Tax Return.
● Instructions for Form 990-T.
● Schedule C (Form 1040), Profit or Loss From Business.
● Schedule F (Form 1040), Profit or Loss From Farming.
● Instructions for Form 1041 and Schedules A, B, D, G, I, J, and K-1, U.S. Income Tax Return for Estates and Trusts.
● Form 1042, Annual Withholding Tax Return for U.S. Source Income of Foreign Persons.
● Instructions for Form 1065, U.S. Return of Partnership Income.
● Instructions for Form 1066, U.S. Real Estate Mortgage Investment Conduit (REMIC) Income Tax Return.
● Instructions for Forms 1120 and 1120-A.
● Form 2553, Election by a Small Business Corporation.
● Form 2848, Power of Attorney and Declaration of Representative.
● Form 8821, Tax Information Authorization.
● Form 8832, Entity Classification Election.

For more information about filing Form SS-4 and related issues, see:
● Pub. 51 (Circular A), Agricultural Employer's Tax Guide;
● Pub. 15 (Circular E), Employer's Tax Guide;
● Pub. 538, Accounting Periods and Methods;
● Pub. 542, Corporations;
● Pub. 557, Tax-Exempt Status for Your Organization;
● Pub. 583, Starting a Business and Keeping Records;
● Pub. 966, The Secure Way to Pay Your Federal Taxes for Business and Individual Taxpayers;
● Pub. 1635, Understanding Your EIN;
● Package 1023, Application for Recognition of Exemption Under Section 501(c)(3) of the Internal Revenue Code; and
● Package 1024, Application for Recognition of Exemption Under Section 501(a).

Specific Instructions

Print or type all entries on Form SS-4. Follow the instructions for each line to expedite processing and to avoid unnecessary IRS requests for additional information. Enter "N/A" (nonapplicable) on the lines that do not apply.

Line 1—Legal name of entity (or individual) for whom the EIN is being requested. Enter the legal name of the entity (or individual) applying for the EIN exactly as it appears on the social security card, charter, or other applicable legal document. An entry is required.

INSTRUCTIONS (CONTINUED) FOR APPLICATION FOR EMPLOYER IDENTIFICATION NUMBER

Individuals. Enter your first name, middle initial, and last name. If you are a sole proprietor, enter your individual name, not your business name. Enter your business name on line 2. Do not use abbreviations or nicknames on line 1.

Trusts. Enter the name of the trust.

Estate of a decedent. Enter the name of the estate. For an estate that has no legal name, enter the name of the decedent followed by "Estate."

Partnerships. Enter the legal name of the partnership as it appears in the partnership agreement.

Corporations. Enter the corporate name as it appears in the corporate charter or other legal document creating it.

Plan administrators. Enter the name of the plan administrator. A plan administrator who already has an EIN should use that number.

Line 2—Trade name of business. Enter the trade name of the business if different from the legal name. The trade name is the "doing business as " (DBA) name.

 Use the full legal name shown on line 1 on all tax returns filed for the entity. (However, if you enter a trade name on line 2 and choose to use the trade name instead of the legal name, enter the trade name on all returns you file.) To prevent processing delays and errors, always use the legal name only (or the trade name only) on all tax returns.

Line 3—Executor, administrator, trustee, "care of" name. Trusts enter the name of the trustee. Estates enter the name of the executor, administrator, or other fiduciary. If the entity applying has a designated person to receive tax information, enter that person's name as the "care of" person. Enter the individual's first name, middle initial, and last name.

Lines 4a-b—Mailing address. Enter the mailing address for the entity's correspondence. If line 3 is completed, enter the address for the executor, trustee or "care of" person. Generally, this address will be used on all tax returns.

 File Form 8822, Change of Address, to report any subsequent changes to the entity's mailing address.

Lines 5a-b—Street address. Provide the entity's physical address only if different from its mailing address shown in lines 4a-b. Do not enter a P.O. box number here.

Line 6—County and state where principal business is located. Enter the entity's primary physical location.

Lines 7a-b—Name of principal officer, general partner, grantor, owner, or trustor. Enter the first name, middle initial, last name, and SSN of (a) the principal officer if the business is a corporation, (b) a general partner if a partnership, (c) the owner of an entity that is disregarded as separate from its owner (disregarded entities owned by a corporation enter the corporation's name and EIN), or (d) a grantor, owner, or trustor if a trust.

If the person in question is an alien individual with a previously assigned individual taxpayer identification number (ITIN), enter the ITIN in the space provided and submit a copy of an official identifying document. If necessary, complete Form W-7, Application for IRS Individual Taxpayer Identification Number, to obtain an ITIN.

You must enter an SSN, ITIN, or EIN unless the only reason you are applying for an EIN is to make an entity classification election (see Regulations sections 301.7701-1 through 301.7701-3) and you are a nonresident alien or other foreign entity with no effectively connected income from sources within the United States.

Line 8a—Type of entity. Check the box that best describes the type of entity applying for the EIN. If you are an alien individual with an ITIN previously assigned to you, enter the ITIN in place of a requested SSN.

 This is not an election for a tax classification of an entity. See Limited liability company (LLC) on page 4.

Other. If not specifically listed, check the "Other" box, enter the type of entity and the type of return, if any, that will be filed (for example, "Common Trust Fund, Form 1065" or "Created a Pension Plan"). Do not enter "N/A." If you are an alien individual applying for an EIN, see the *Lines 7a-b* instructions above.

• **Household employer.** If you are an individual, check the "Other" box and enter "Household Employer" and your SSN. If you are a state or local agency serving as a tax reporting agent for public assistance recipients who become household employers, check the "Other" box and enter "Household Employer Agent." If you are a trust that qualifies as a household employer, you do not need a separate EIN for reporting tax information relating to household employees; use the EIN of the trust.

• **QSub.** For a qualified subchapter S subsidiary (QSub) check the "Other" box and specify "QSub."

• **Withholding agent.** If you are a withholding agent required to file Form 1042, check the "Other" box and enter "Withholding Agent."

Sole proprietor. Check this box if you file Schedule C, C-EZ, or F (Form 1040) and have a qualified plan, or are required to file excise, employment, alcohol, tobacco, or firearms returns, or are a payer of gambling winnings. Enter your SSN (or ITIN) in the space provided. If you are a nonresident alien with no effectively connected income from sources within the United States, you do not need to enter an SSN or ITIN.

Corporation. This box is for any corporation other than a personal service corporation. If you check this box, enter the income tax form number to be filed by the entity in the space provided.

 If you entered "1120S" after the "Corporation" checkbox, the corporation must file Form 2553 no later than the 15th day of the 3rd month of the tax year the election is to take effect. Until Form 2553 has been received and approved, you will be considered a Form 1120 filer. See the Instructions for Form 2553.

Personal service corporation. Check this box if the entity is a personal service corporation. An entity is a personal service corporation for a tax year only if:
• The principal activity of the entity during the testing period (prior tax year) for the tax year is the performance of personal services substantially by employee-owners, and
• The employee-owners own at least 10% of the fair market value of the outstanding stock in the entity on the last day of the testing period.

Personal services include performance of services in such fields as health, law, accounting, or consulting. For more information about personal service corporations,

-3-

INSTRUCTIONS (CONTINUED) FOR APPLICATION FOR EMPLOYER IDENTIFICATION NUMBER

10. Put in this area the date you will start the venture.

11. If sole proprietor, partnership or S Corporation, fill in "December." If C Corporation, consult your tax advisor.

12–15. Self-explanatory.

16a. Usually the answer is NO.

Be sure to print your name and title, include your telephone number, sign the form, and date it before mailing.

The SS-4 application may be downloaded from the IRS web site. You may also apply on line by visiting the IRS site and clicking on the left at: Online EIN Application. Complete the form and click at submit.

COMPLETING THE STATE OF NEW JERSEY FORM NJ REG
(Application for Business Registration and Sales Tax)

This particular application is similar to the SS4 form because it alerts the State of New Jersey to the fact that you are in business. The information requested is basically the same as the federal form, but goes one step further. The rear of this form alerts the State to the fact that you will be responsible for sales tax. The form should be filed by all new businesses including sole proprietorships, partnerships and corporations.

The front of the registration form with letters A–N are questions of a general nature about the business and its owner(s). Letters I and J require that you refer to the State's instruction form to fill in the proper codes.

The back of this form asks questions about sales tax, employees and various license requirements. Be sure to answer all the questions since the State will forward to you the sales filing data and employee withholding tables.

The addresses of the New Jersey Sales Tax Offices are noted on page 43. If you place a call to any of these locations, they will gladly mail you the necessary applications or you may write to the:

Division of Taxation
Information Section
CN 999
Trenton, New Jersey 08625

For registration information, the phone numbers are:
(609) 292-1730, (609) 292-6400, 1-(800) 323-4400.

STATE OF NEW JERSEY
DIVISION OF REVENUE
BUSINESS REGISTRATION APPLICATION

NJ-REG
(8-06)

Please read instructions carefully before filling out this form
ALL SECTIONS MUST BE FULLY COMPLETED

* NO FEE REQUIRED *

MAIL TO:
CLIENT REGISTRATION
PO BOX 252
TRENTON, NJ 08646-0252

OVERNIGHT DELIVERY:
CLIENT REGISTRATION
847 ROEBLING AVENUE
TRENTON, NJ 08611

FAX:
(609) 292-4291

REGISTRATION DETAIL

A. Please indicate the reason for your filing this application (Check only <u>one</u> box)
- ☐ Original application for a new business
- ☐ Application for a new location of an existing registered business
- ☐ Amended application for an existing business
- ☐ Moved previously registered business to new location (REG-C-L can be used in lieu of NJ-REG)
- ☐ Applying for a Business Registration Certificate

Name and NJ Registration Number of your existing business:_____

B. FEIN # `2` `2` `2` `2` `2` `2` `2` `2` OR Soc. Sec. # of Owner ☐☐☐ ☐☐ ☐☐☐☐
☐ Check Box if "Applied for"

C. Name JON and AMY CARLIN
(If INCORPORATED - give Corp. Name; If NOT - give Last Name; First Name, MI of Owner, Partners)

D. Trade Name JAMY'S DONUT SHOPPE

E. Business Location: (Do not use P.O. Box for Location Address)

Street 44 DONNA COURT

City CLARK   State N J

Zip Code `0` `7` `0` `6` `6` `1` `2` `3` `4`
(Give 9-digit Zip)
(See instructions for providing alternate addresses)

F. Mailing Name and Address: (if different from business address)

Name_____

Street_____

City_____ State ☐☐

Zip Code ☐☐☐☐☐ ☐☐☐☐
(Give 9-digit Zip)

BUSINESS DETAIL

G. Beginning date for this business: 1 / 1 / 07 (see instructions)
month   day   year

O/C ___

H. Type of ownership (check one):
- ☐ NJ Corporation   ☐ Sole Proprietor   ☒ Partnership   ☐ Out-of-State Corporation   ☐ LLP   ☐ Other_____
- ☐ Limited Partnership   ☐ LLC (1065 Filer)   ☐ LLC (1120 Filer)   ☐ LLC (Single Member)   ☐ S Corporation (You **must** complete page 41)

I. New Jersey Business Code `5` `3` `0` `6` (see instructions)

J. County / Municipality Code `2` `0` `0` `2` (see instructions) K. County UNION
(New Jersey only)

FOR OFFICIAL USE ONLY

DLN _____

CORP # _____

L. Will this business be open all year? ☒ Yes ☐ No
If NO - Circle months business will be open:

JAN   FEB   MAR   APR   MAY   JUN   JUL   AUG   SEPT   OCT   NOV   DEC

M. IF A CORPORATION, complete the following:

Date of Incorporation: _____ / _____ / _____
month   day   year

State of Incorporation ☐☐   Fiscal month ☐☐

Is this a Subsidiary of another corporation? ☐ YES ☐ NO   NJ Business/Corp. # ☐☐☐☐ ☐☐☐☐ ☐☐☐

If YES, give name and Federal ID# of parent: _____

N. Standard Industrial Code ☐☐☐☐ (If known)   O. NAICS ☐☐☐☐☐☐ (If known)

P. Provide the following information for the owner, partners or responsible corporate officers. (If more space is needed, attach rider)

OWNERSHIP DETAIL

NAME (Last Name, First, MI)	SOCIAL SECURITY NUMBER / TITLE	HOME ADDRESS (Street, City, State, Zip)	PERCENT OF OWNERSHIP
CARLIN, JON	111-11-1111	26 EAST WAY, LINCROFT	50
	PARTNER	NEW JERSEY 07738	
CARLIN, AMY	222-22-2222	26 EAST WAY, LINCROFT	50
	PARTNER	NEW JERSEY 07738	

BE SURE TO COMPLETE NEXT PAGE

APPLICATION TO REGISTER A BUSINESS
IN NEW JERSEY

FEIN#: _____   NAME: JON and AMY CARLIN _____   **NJ-REG**

Each Question Must Be Answered Completely

1. a. Have you or will you be paying wages, salaries or commissions to employees working in New Jersey within the next 6 months? .... ☐ Yes ☒ No

   Give date of first wage or salary payment: _____ / _____ / _____
   Month   Day   Year

   If you answered "No" to question 1.a., please be aware that if you begin paying wages you are required to notify the Client Registration Bureau
   at PO Box 252, Trenton NJ 08646-0252, or phone (609)-292-1730.

   b. Give date of hiring first NJ employee: _____ / _____ / _____
   Month   Day   Year

   c. Date cumulative gross payroll exceeds $1,000 _____ / _____ / _____
   Month   Day   Year

   d. Will you be paying wages, salaries or commissions to New Jersey residents working outside New Jersey? .... ☐ Yes ☒ No

   e. Will you be the payer of pension or annuity income to New Jersey residents? .... ☐ Yes ☒ No

   f. Will you be holding legalized games of chance in New Jersey (as defined in Chapter 47 Rules of Legalized Games of Chance) where
   proceeds from any one prize exceed $1,000? .... ☐ Yes ☒ No

   g. Is this business a PEO (Employee Leasing Company)?   (If yes, see page 6) .... ☐ Yes ☒ No

2. Did you acquire ☐ Substantially all the assets; ☐ Trade or business; ☐ Employees; of any previous employing units? .... ☐ Yes ☒ No
   If answer is "No", go to question 4.
   If answer is "Yes", indicate by a check whether ☐ in whole or ☐ in part, and list business name, address and registration number of predecessor
   or acquired unit and the date business was acquired by you. (If more than one, list separately. Continue on separate sheet if necessary.)

   Name of Acquired Unit _____   _____
   _____   _____   N.J. Employer ID

   Address _____   _____
   _____   _____   Date Acquired

	PERCENTAGE ACQUIRED
ACQUIRED	
☐ Assets	_____%
☐ Trade or Business	_____%
☐ Employees	_____%

3. Subject to certain regulations, the law provides for the transfer of the predecessor's employment experience to a successor where the whole of a business is acquired
   from a subject predecessor employer. The transfer of the employment experience is required by law.

   Are the predecessor and successor units owned or controlled by the same interests? .... ☐ Yes ☒ No

4. Is your employment agricultural? .... ☐ Yes ☒ No

5. Is your employment household? .... ☐ Yes ☒ No

   a. If yes, please indicate the date in the calendar quarter in which gross cash wages totaled $1,000 or more _____ / _____ / _____
   Month   Day   Year

6. Are you a 501(c)(3) organization? .... ☐ Yes ☒ No

7. Were you subject to the Federal Unemployment Tax Act (FUTA) in the current or preceding calendar year? .... ☐ Yes ☒ No

   (See instruction sheet for explanation of FUTA) If "Yes", indicate year: _____

8. a. Does this employing unit claim exemption from liability for contributions under the Unemployment Compensation Law of New Jersey? ..... ☐ Yes ☒ No

   If "Yes", please state reason. (Use additional sheets if necessary.) _____

   b. If exemption from the mandatory provisions of the Unemployment Compensation Law of New Jersey is claimed, does this employing unit
   wish to voluntarily elect to become subject to its provisions for a period of not less than two complete calendar years? .... ☐ Yes ☒ No

9. Type of business   ☐ 1. Manufacturer   ☐ 2. Service   ☐ 3. Wholesale
                         ☐ 4. Construction   ☒ 5. Retail   ☐ 6. Government

   Principal product or service in New Jersey only BAKED GOODS
   Type of Activity in New Jersey only BAKERY

10. List below each place of business and each class of industry in New Jersey, even though you may have only one place of business or
    engage in only one class of industry.

    a. Do you have more than one employing facility in New Jersey .... ☐ Yes ☒ No

NJ WORK LOCATIONS (Physical location, not mailing address)		NATURE OF BUSINESS (See Instructions)			No. of Workers a Each Location and/in Each Clas of Industry
Street Address, City, Zip Code	County	NAICS Code	Principal Product or Service Complete Description	%	
44 DONNA COURT, CLARK, NJ 07066	UNION	5306	BAKED GOODS	100	NON

(Continue on separate sheet, if necessary)
BE SURE TO COMPLETE NEXT PAGE

APPLICATION TO REGISTER A BUSINESS
IN NEW JERSEY
(CONTINUED)

FEIN: _____ NAME: JON and AMY CARLIN _____

Each Question Must Be Answered Completely

11. a. Will you collect New Jersey Sales Tax and/or pay Use Tax? .... ☒ Yes ☐ No
     GIVE EXACT DATE YOU EXPECT TO MAKE FIRST SALE __2__ / __1__ / __07__
                                  Month   Day   Year

     b. Will you need to make exempt purchases for your inventory or to produce your product? .... ☒ Yes ☐ No

     c. Is your business located in (check applicable box(es)): ☐ Atlantic City ☐ Salem County
                                             ☐ North Wildwood ☐ Wildwood Crest ☐ Wildwood

     d. Do you have more than one location in New Jersey that collects New Jersey Sales Tax? (If yes, see instructions) ...... ☐ Yes ☒ No

     e. Do you, in the regular course of business, sell, store, deliver or transport natural gas or electricity to users or customers
        in this state whether by mains, lines or pipes located within this State or by any other means of delivery? .... ☐ Yes ☒ No

12. Do you intend to sell cigarettes? .... ☐ Yes ☒ No
    Note: If yes, complete the REG-L form on page 45 in this booklet and return with your completed NJ-REG.
    To obtain a cigarette retail or vending machine license complete and return the form CM-100 on page 47.

13. a. Are you a **distributor** or **wholesaler** of tobacco products other than cigarettes? .... ☐ Yes ☒ No

     b. Do you purchase tobacco products other than cigarettes from outside the State of New Jersey? .... ☐ Yes ☒ No

14. Are you a manufacturer, wholesaler, distributor or retailer of "litter-generating products"? See instructions for retailer .... ☐ Yes ☒ No
    liability and definition of litter-generating products.

15. Are you an owner or operator of a sanitary landfill facility in New Jersey? .... ☐ Yes ☒ No
    IF YES, indicate D.E.P. Facility # and type (See instructions) _____

16. a. Do you operate a facility that has the total combined capacity to store 200,000 gallons or more of petroleum products? .. ☐ Yes ☒ No

     b. Do you operate a facility that has the total combined capacity to store 20,000 gallons
        (equals 167,043 pounds) of hazardous chemicals? .... ☐ Yes ☒ No

     c. Do you store petroleum products or hazardous chemicals at a public storage terminal? .... ☐ Yes ☒ No
        Name of terminal _____

17. a. Will you be involved with the sale or transport of motor fuels and/or petroleum? .... ☐ Yes ☒ No
     Note: If yes, complete the REG-L form in this booklet and return with your completed NJ-REG.
     To obtain a motor fuels retail or transport license complete and return the CM-100 in this booklet.

     b. Will your company be engaged in the refining and/or distributing of petroleum products for distribution in this State or
        the importing of petroleum products into New Jersey for consumption in New Jersey? .... ☐ Yes ☒ No

     c. Will your business activity require you to issue a Direct Payment Permit in lieu of payment of the Petroleum Products
        Gross Receipts Tax on your purchases of petroleum products? .... ☐ Yes ☒ No

18. Will you be providing goods and services as a direct contractor or subcontractor to the state, other public agencies
    including local governments, colleges and universities and school boards, or to casino licensees? .... ☐ Yes ☒ No

19. Will you be engaged in the business of renting motor vehicles for the transportation of persons
    or non-commercial freight? .... ☐ Yes ☒ No

20. Is your business a hotel, motel, bed & breakfast or similar facility and located in the State of New Jersey? .... ☐ Yes ☒ No

21. Do you hold a permit or license, issued by the New Jersey Department of Transportation, to erect and maintain
    an outdoor advertising sign or to engage in the business of outdoor advertising? .... ☐ Yes ☒ No

22. Do you make retail sales of new motor vehicle tires, or sell or lease motor vehicles? .... ☐ Yes ☒ No

23. Do you provide "cosmetic medical procedures" or goods or occupancies directly associated with such procedures? .... ☐ Yes ☒ No
    (See description of Cosmetic Procedures Gross Receipts Tax in the list of Taxes of the State of New Jersey, page 5.)
    Type of Business _____

24. Do you sell voice grade access telecommunications or mobile telecommunications to a customer with a primary
    place of use in this State? .... ☐ Yes ☒ No

25. Will you make retail sales of "fur clothing"? .... ☐ Yes ☒ No
    (See full description of Fur Clothing Retail Gross Receipts Tax in the list of Taxes of the State of New Jersey, page 5)

26. Contact Information: Person AMY CARLIN _____ Title: PARTNER _____

    Daytime Phone: (___) _____ - _____ Ext. _____ E-mail address: ACARLIN@YAHOO.COM _____

    Signature of Owner, Partner or Officer: *Amy Carlin* _____

    Title PARTNER _____ Date: 1/1/07 _____

NO FEE IS REQUIRED TO FILE THIS FORM

IF YOU ARE A SOLE PROPRIETOR OR A PARTNERSHIP WITHOUT EMPLOYEES - **STOP HERE** -
IF YOU HAVE EMPLOYEES PROCEED TO THE STATE OF NJ NEW HIRE REPORTING FORM ON PAGE 29

IF YOU ARE FORMING A CORPORATION, LIMITED LIABILITY COMPANY, LIMITED PARTNERSHIP, OR A LIMITED
LIABILITY PARTNERSHIP YOU MUST CONTINUE ANSWERING APPLICABLE QUESTIONS ON PAGES 23 AND 24

APPLICATION TO REGISTER A BUSINESS
IN NEW JERSEY
(CONTINUED)

INSTRUCTIONS
BUSINESS REGISTRATION FORM (NJ-REG)

The NJ Division of Revenue adopted this registration procedure to assist you in becoming aware of and understanding all of the taxes and related liabilities to which a new business or applicant for a license may be subject. The procedure covers tax/employer registration for ALL types of businesses, and also covers the filing of NEW legal business entities such as domestic/foreign corporations or limited liability companies (Public Records Filing, page 23-24).

All businesses must complete the registration application (NJ-REG, pages 17-19) in order to receive the forms, returns, instructions, and other information needed to comply with New Jersey laws. This applies to every individual, corporation, or other legal business entity, or unincorporated entity engaged in the conduct or practice of any trade, business, profession, or occupation, whether full time or part time, within the State of New Jersey. Registration requirements also apply to name holder and dormant corporations, as well as to owners of tangible personal property used in business located in New Jersey or leased to another business entity in New Jersey. **Nonprofit "501(c)(3)" or veteran's organizations that need to apply for sales tax exemption ONLY must complete the application for an Exempt Organization Certificate (REG-1E) instead of the NJ-REG and mail it to the Division of Taxation for approval.** Persons commencing business or opening additional places of business must register at least 15 business days prior to commencement or opening. There is no fee for filing NJ-REG; however, as outlined in the instructions, there are fees for filing new business entities.

Mail the completed NJ-REG to:

NEW JERSEY DIVISION OF REVENUE
PO BOX 252
TRENTON, NEW JERSEY 08646-0252

Overnight Delivery of NJ-REG to:

NEW JERSEY DIVISION OF REVENUE
847 ROEBLING AVENUE
TRENTON, NJ 08611

To submit a Public Records Filing or combined Public Records Filing with NJ-REG, refer to page 21 (Items 2 a-c).

IMPORTANT- READ THE FOLLOWING INSTRUCTIONS CAREFULLY BEFORE COMPLETING ANY FORMS. PRINT OR TYPE ALL INFORMATION. PROVIDE A COMPLETE APPLICATION. FAILURE TO PROPERLY COMPLETE THE APPLICATION MAY DELAY ISSUANCE OF YOUR CERTIFICATE OF AUTHORITY OR LICENSE.

PAGE 17 INSTRUCTIONS -

Item A   Check the appropriate box to indicate reason for filing the application. Check only **one** box. Nonprofits that are 501(c)(3), volunteer fire or parent-teacher organizations and want to apply for exemption from sales tax need to file Form REG-1-E, instead of the NJ-REG. The form is available by calling (609) 292-5995.

Item B   Enter the FEIN assigned to the employer or vendor by the Internal Revenue Service or if not required, enter the Social Security Number assigned to the sole proprietor. Check the box if you have applied for your FEIN.

Item C   Enter the corporate name of the business being registered or the name(s) of the owner(s) if an individual or partnership.

Item D   Enter the Trade Name, if different from Item C.

Item E   Enter the address of the **physical** location of the business, do not use a PO Box address. Be sure to include the **nine-digit zip-code.**

Item F   Enter the name and address to which **all** New Jersey tax returns will be mailed. Be sure to include the nine-digit zip code. If you wish different type tax returns to go to different addresses, please attach a separate sheet and indicate the address to which each tax return is to go.

Item G   Enter the date which you started or assumed ownership of this business in New Jersey. If your business has not yet started, enter the date that you will commence doing business. If no business is conducted in NJ, but, you are going to withhold NJ Gross Income Tax for employees, enter the date withholding will begin. Use today's date if you only need a Business Registration Certificate.

Item H   Check the appropriate box for your Type of Ownership. If you check "S Corporation," complete the New Jersey S Corporation Election form (CBT-2553) found in this booklet on page 41.

Item I   Enter your New Jersey Business Code from Table A. If you are engaged in more than one type of business, enter the code for the predominant one. **This section must be completed to avoid delays in issuance of the Certificate of Authority or License.**

Item J   Enter your New Jersey County/Municipality Code from Table B. This code reflects the County/Municipality in which your business is located.

Item K   Enter the county where your business is located.

Item L   If this business will be open all year, check the "YES" box. If this is a seasonal business, check "NO" and indicate the months the business is **open.**

Item M   If the business is a corporation, enter the date and state of incorporation, the fiscal month of the corporation and the NJ

corporation business number of the corporation. If this business is a subsidiary of another corporation, check "YES" and enter the name and FEIN of the parent.

Item N   Enter the four-digit Standard Industrial Code (SIC) if known.

Item O   Enter the six-digit North American Industrial Classification System Code (NAICS) if known. (See Table C, page 14)

Item P   Enter the names of the owner, partners or responsible corporate officer(s). Enter the social security number, title, and home address for each person listed.

PAGE 18 INSTRUCTIONS -

Question 1:

(a)   Have you or will you be paying wages, salaries or commissions to employees working in New Jersey within the next 6 months, check "YES" and enter the date of the first payment. This date must be provided for Unemployment and Disability registration purposes. If "NO", please be aware that if you begin paying wages you are required to notify the Client Registration Bureau at (609)-292-1730.

(b)   If 1(a) is "YES", enter the date you hired your 1st New Jersey employee.

(c)   This date must be provided for Unemployment and Disability registration purposes. Accumulate the gross periodic payrolls until they add up to a total of $1,000. Enter that date on line 1c.

(d)   If you will be paying wages, salaries or commissions to New Jersey residents working outside New Jersey, check "YES".

(e)   If you will be the payer of pensions and/or annuities to New Jersey residents, check "YES" and enter the date of the first payment.

(f)   If you will be holding legalized games of chance in New Jersey (as defined in Chapter 47 "Rules of Legalized Games of Chance") where proceeds from any one prize exceed $1,000, check "YES" and enter the date of the first prize awarded. (NJ Lottery proceeds are not included.)

(g)   A PEO (Employee Leasing Company) that registers with the NJ Division of Revenue via NJ-REG is subject to an **additional** and **separate** registration process with the **NJ Department of Labor.** To obtain the special PEO registration forms and information, please visit our website, www.state.nj.us/labor/ea/eaindex.html or call 609-633-6400 x 2209.

Question 2:

If you purchased or otherwise came into possession of 90% or more of the assets of another business, check "Substantially all the assets". If you purchased or otherwise received the right to continue to operate the entire trade or business of another employer, check "Trade or Business". If you took over all the employees of an existing business, excluding corporate officers if any, check "Employees".

INSTRUCTIONS FOR
APPLICATION TO REGISTER A BUSINESS
IN NEW JERSEY

Enter the name, any trade name and address of the business you acquired. Also enter the New Jersey Unemployment Registration Number or FEIN of the prior business as well as the date you purchased the business. Also indicate the percentage of assets, trade or business and employees that you took over from the prior business.

Question 3:
When the successor acquires or absorbs and continues the business of a subject predecessor, the successor employer must receive the transfer of the predecessor's employment experience. The transfer of employment experience is required by law.

Question 4: Agricultural labor means the following activities:
1. Services performed on a farm in connection with cultivation of the soil; raising or harvesting any agricultural or horticultural product; raising, feeding, caring for and managing livestock, bees, poultry or fur-bearing animals; handling, packaging, or processing any agricultural or horticultural commodity in its unmanufactured state; repair and maintenance of equipment or real property used in the agricultural activity; and transport of agricultural or horticultural supplies or products if not in the usual course of a trucking business;

2. Service performed in a greenhouse or nursery if over 50 percent of the gross sales volume is attributable to products raised in the greenhouse or nursery; and

3. Service performed by a cooperative of which the producer of the agricultural product is a member if the service performed is incidental and necessary to the delivery of the product to market in a finished state.

   Agricultural labor does not include:
   1. Service performed at a race track;

   2. Service in the breeding, care or boarding of domesticated animals of a kind normally found in a home, such as dogs and cats;

   3. Service in a retail enterprise selling the product of an agricultural enterprise if the retail enterprise is not located on or contiguous to the site of production; or

   4. Service in a retail enterprise located on or contiguous to the site of production if greater than 50% of the gross sales volume of the retail enterprise is attributable to items not produced at the site.

Question 5:
Household service means service of a personal nature performed outside of a business enterprise for a householder. Household service is normally performed in a private residence, but may be performed in other settings such as a nursing home or a yacht. Household service would include, but is not limited to, the following occupations: maids, butlers, cooks, valets, gardeners, chauffeurs; personal secretaries, baby-sitters and nurses' aides.

(a) If "YES", this date is to be provided for Unemployment and Disability registration purposes. Accumulate the gross periodic cash payrolls until they add up to a total of $1,000 in a calendar quarter. Enter that date here.

Question 6:
Has the Internal Revenue Service determined that your organization is exempt from income tax as a 501(c)(3) organization? If yes, check "YES".

Question 7:
Any employing unit subject to the provisions of the Federal Unemployment Tax Act (FUTA) in the current or preceding calendar year automatically becomes an employer unless services are specifically excluded under the New Jersey Unemployment Law. An employing unit (other than one which employs agricultural workers) is generally subject to FUTA if it had covered employment during some portion of a day in 20 different calendar weeks within the calendar year or had a quarterly payroll of $1,500 or more.

Question 8:
If you believe that you or your business is not required to pay unemployment and temporary disability contributions on wages paid to its employees, check "YES", otherwise check "NO". Examples are: This is a church or the only employees of this proprietorship are the spouse and children under age 18. You may be subject to New Jersey Gross Income Tax Withholding.

Question 9:
For principal product or service in New Jersey only, please provide a description for that product or service which accounts for over 50% of your business (i.e. fuel oil). Please briefly describe the type of activity your business is engaged in (i.e. drive a fuel truck to sell fuel oil to consumers).

Question 10:
This information is to be supplied by every employer regardless of the number of work locations in New Jersey or the number of classes of industry which it is engaged in. Please do not describe work location by post office box number. The incorporated municipalities in which workers operate or to which they report daily should be named instead. If there is more than one location please list each location beginning with the largest employing facility first. Please provide the location address and indicate the nature of business conducted at each location. If two or more principal classes of activity are conducted at one location, please indicate.

In describing the "Nature of Business", classify your "Primary Activity" under one of the following: wholesale trade, retail trade, manufacturing, mining and quarrying, construction (general or specific), real estate, insurance, finance, transportation, communication, or other public utilities, personal service, business service, professional service, agriculture, forestry, fishery. If the employing unit is engaged in trade, state under "Primary Activity" whether as wholesaler, commission merchant or wholesale branch of manufacturing concern, retailer (store, route, restaurant, fast food, service station, and the like), or retail branch of manufacturing concern. Please refer to the list of business codes provided.

For units engaged in manufacturing, state the product which has the greatest gross annual value. Describe also the basic raw materials or articles. For units with more than one principal product or service show percentage of gross value in each.

For contractors (subcontractors) in construction, state the type of activity, such as general (building or other), highway, heavy marine (not ship), water well, demolition, or specific (i.e. plumbing, painting, masonry or stone, carpentry, roofing, concrete, general maintenance construction and the like), speculative builder, development builder.

For service providers, state whether hotel, laundry, photography, barber or beauty, funeral, garment, hygienic, business janitor, news, radio, accounting, educational, repair, entertainment, amusement, athletic specific professional or the like.

For the wholesaler or retailer, describe primary commodity.

If engaged in marine transportation, state whether on inland water-ways, harbors, coastwise or trans-oceanic.

For employers engaged in more than one business activity (i.e. service station, mini-mart) show (in the percent column) the relative gross business each activity does.

The average number of employees on the payroll at each location and in each class of activity should be shown. Please continue on a separate sheet if needed.

PAGE 19 INSTRUCTIONS
Question 11
(a) If you will be collecting New Jersey Sales Tax and/or paying Use Tax check "YES" and enter the date of the first sale.
(b) Check "YES" if you will be making tax exempt purchases. If "YES", you will be issued New Jersey Resale Certificates (ST-3) and/or Exempt Use Certificates (ST-4).

   NOTE: Form ST-3, Resale Certificate. Issued to a vendor by a purchaser who is not the "end user" of the goods or services being purchased.

   Form ST-4, Exempt Use Certificate. Issued to a vendor by a purchaser who is purchasing goods for an exempt use.

(c) If your business is located within Atlantic City, Salem County, North Wildwood, Wildwood Crest or Wildwood, check the applicable box.

   If you are eligible for the New York/New Jersey Cooperative Interstate Sales Tax Agreement, indicate this in Question 18 under "Other State Taxes".

(d) All NJ locations collecting NJ sales tax must be registered. If "YES", attach a rider requesting consolidated reporting.

(e) If you sell, store, deliver or transport natural gas or electricity to users or customers whether by mains, lines, or pipes located within this State or by any other means of delivery, check "YES".

INSTRUCTIONS FOR
APPLICATION TO REGISTER A BUSINESS
IN NEW JERSEY
(CONTINUED)

Question 12:
If you intend to sell cigarettes in New Jersey, check "YES". If "YES", complete Form REG-L if you are requesting a wholesaler, distributor or manufacturer license application. Complete Form CM-100 if you are applying for a retailer or vending machine license.You will be sent the appropriate license/license application after these forms are processed.

Question 13:
(a) If you are a distributor or wholesaler of tobacco products other than cigarettes, check "YES". Examples of tobacco products are: cigars, little cigars, cigarillos, chewing tobacco, pipe tobacco, smoking tobacco, tobacco substitutes and snuff. Cigarettes are exempt from the Tobacco Products Wholesale Sales and Use Tax.

(b) If the distributor or wholesaler has not collected the Tobacco Products Wholesale Sales and Use Tax from the retailer or consumer, the retailer or consumer is responsible for remitting the compensating use tax on the price paid or charged directly to the Division of Taxation within 20 days of the date the tax was required to be paid.

Question 14:
If you are a manufacturer, wholesaler, distributor or retailer of "litter-generating products", check "YES". Litter-generating products are: food, soft drinks and carbonated water, beer, wine, distilled spirits, glass containers, metal containers, plastic or fiber containers, groceries, drugstore sundries, cigarettes and tobacco products, motor vehicle tires, newsprint and magazine paper stock, paper products and household paper, and cleaning agents and toiletries.

Question 15:
If you are an owner or operator of a sanitary landfill facility in New Jersey, check "YES" and indicate the facility number and type as classified by the New Jersey Department of Environmental Protection. Registration instructions for the Solid Waste Services and Landfill Closure and Contingency taxes will be forwarded.

Question 16:
(a) If you operate a facility that has the total combined capacity to store 200,000 gallons or more of petroleum products, check "YES".

(b) If you operate a facility that has the total combined capacity to store 20,000 gallons of hazardous chemicals, check "YES".

(c) If you store petroleum products or hazardous chemicals at a public storage terminal, check "YES", and enter the name of the terminal. A Spill Compensation and Control Tax registration application will be forwarded.

Question 17:
(a) If your company will be involved with the sale or transport of motor fuels and/or petroleum, check "YES". If "YES", complete Form REG-L if you are requesting a wholesaler, distributor, import, export, seller/use, gasoline jobber, or storage facility operator license application. Complete Form CM-100 if you are applying for a retail dealer or transport license. You will be sent the appropriate license/license application after these forms are processed.

(b) If your company is engaged in refining and/or distributing petroleum products for distribution in this State, or importing petroleum products into New Jersey for consumption in New Jersey, check "YES". If you have checked "YES", complete Form REG-L and return it with your competed NJ-REG.

(c) If you checked "YES", you will be sent a Direct Payment Permit application.

Question 18:
If you will be providing goods or services to casino licensees or acting as a contractor or subcontractor to the State or its agencies, check the "YES" box.

Question 19:
Businesses involved in the rental of motor vehicles (less than 28 day agreements), including passenger autos, trucks and trailers designed for use on the highways, other than those used for the transportation of commercial freight, are subject to the payment of a $2 per day Domestic Security Fee. If eligible, a business must check YES and go to http://www.state.nj.us/treasury/taxation/prntmisc.htm for instructions on how to report and pay the fee quarterly either electronically or by phone (Form DSF-100). See Technical Bulletin 47(R) on this topic at: http://www.state.nj.us/treasury/taxation/publtb.htm.

Question 20:
Businesses engaged in the rental of rooms in a hotel, motel, bed & breakfast or similar facility are required to collect a State Occupancy Fee of 5% as of 7-1-04. In addition, a Municipal Occupancy Tax of up to 3% must also be collected, if enacted by the municipality where the facility is located. If such a facility, check YES. You will receive the HM-100 return, which must be filed with payment by the 20th of each month. For additional information on the Fee and a list of municipalities that have enacted the Tax, go to: http://www.state.nj.us/treasury/taxation/hotelfeeinfo.htm.

Question 21:
Businesses that hold an outdoor advertising license or permit issued by the New Jersey DOT are subject to the 6% Outdoor Advertising Fee imposed on gross amounts collected for the sale of advertising space. If you have such a license or permit, check YES. You will receive the OA-100 return which is due on a quarterly basis. For additional information on the Fee, go to: www.state.nj.us/treasury/taxation.

Question 22:
If you sell new tires, or sell or lease motor vehicles, you must check YES. You will receive information regarding the collection of the Motor Vehicle Tire Fee.

Question 23:
If you provide such services, check YES and indicate the type of business, service or practice you are engaged in (e.g. plastic surgery, electrolysis, beauty salon/spa, hair replacement facility, hospital)

Question 24:
If you are a telephone exchange company or a mobile telecommunications carrier which provides voice grade access telephone numbers or service lines as part of that telephone exchange service, thereby providing access to 9-1-1 service through the public switched network, you must check YES. You will receive the ERF-100 return which is due on a quarterly basis.

Question 25:
"Fur clothing" means an item that satisfies the following criteria: Its sale is exempt from sales tax under the "clothing" exemption of the Sales and Use Tax Act and fur is a chief component of its value. "Fur" means fur on the hide or pelt of an animal.

Question 26:
Contact Person: Enter the name, title, telephone number and e-mail address of the contact person who will answer questions regarding the registration application.

Signature: The application **must be signed and dated** by the owner if a sole proprietorship, or in the case of a corporation, by the president, vice-president, secretary, treasurer, comptroller, or other duly authorized officer. Unsigned applications cannot be processed and will be returned.

INSTRUCTIONS FOR
APPLICATION TO REGISTER A BUSINESS
IN NEW JERSEY
(CONTINUED)

TABLE A - NEW JERSEY BUSINESS CODES
Enter one of the following four-digit numbers in Block I to indicate the product group or service of your business:

MISCELLANEOUS WITHHOLDER CODES

Code	Description
2781	Pension Plan Withholders
2779	Employer of Domestic Household Employees

MANUFACTURING BUSINESS CODES

Code	Description
1631	Aircraft and Related Supplies
1314	Alcoholic Beverages/Liquor
1100	Apparel
1404	Appliances, Housewares, Linens
1622	Art, Mechanical Drawing & Related Supplies
1815	Asphalt
1405	Audio/Visual (TV, Stereo, Records, CD)
1208	Auto Parts and Related Products/Accessories
1220	Auto Windows/Glass
1200	Automotive
1306	Baked Goods
1637	Bicycles and Related Merchandise
1604	Books, Magazines, Periodicals, Newspapers
1316	Bottled Water
1809	Building Materials and Supplies
1800	Building/Construction
1213	Buses, Bus Parts
1614	Cameras, Photo Equipment and Supplies
1304	Candy, Nuts and Confectionary
1104	Children's & Infants' Clothing and/or Accessories
1602	Computer Hardware, Software
1808	Concrete
1627	Containers (Industrial/Commercial)
1110	Costumes
1107	Custom Clothing and Tailoring
1305	Dairy Products
1601	Drugs & Medical Supplies, Medical Equipment
1502	Dry Goods
1903	Electric
1905	Electric and Gas
1804	Electrical Materials
1630	Electronic Equipment
1812	Energy Conservation Related
1105	Family Clothing
1607	Farm and Garden Equipment and Supplies
1823	Fencing
1611	Flowers and Related Merchandise
1300	Food
1106	Footwear
1103	Formal Wear (Tuxedos, Bridal Gowns, etc.)
1303	Fruit and/or Vegetables
1609	Fuel (Bottled Gas, Kerosene, Charcoal, etc.)
1400	Furniture
1108	Furriers
1904	Gas
1500	General Merchandise
1615	Gifts, Souvenirs
1301	Grocery Items
1634	Hair Grooming Supplies
1813	Hardware
1315	Health Food Products
1810	Heating, Ventilation and Air Conditioning
1401	Household Furniture and Furnishings
1610	Ice
1311	Ice Cream Products
1619	Industrial Supplies
1618	Industrial Tools and Equipment, Machinery
1820	Iron and Steel
1608	Jewelry
1406	Lamps, Lights, Shades
1617	Leather Goods and Luggage
1814	Lumber
1302	Meat and /or Fish
1101	Men's and Boys' Clothing and/or Accessories
1111	Millinery and Accessories
1626	Miscellaneous Decorative & Display Materials
1600	Miscellaneous Products
1621	Models and Hobby Related Merchandise
1638	Monuments, Caskets & Related Merchandise
1201	Motor Vehicles

Code	Description
1207	Motorboats
1209	Motorcycles, Minibikes
1215	Mufflers
1606	Musical Instruments & Related Merchandise
1318	Non-Alcoholic Beverages
1402	Office Furniture and Furnishings
1616	Optical Goods
1803	Paint, Wallpaper and Decorating
1633	Paintings, Sculpture and Related Artwork
1628	Paper and Packaging Products
1635	Perfumes and Cosmetics
1640	Pet Supplies
1313	Pizza
1802	Plumbing Materials
1623	Pools and Related Accessories
1202	Recreational Vehicles, Campers
1807	Roofing Materials
1822	Siding (Aluminum, Brickface, Stucco)
1620	Signs and Advertising Displays
1636	Soaps, Detergents, etc.
1307	Specialty Foods
1605	Sporting Goods and Related Merchandise
1603	Stamps, Coins, Gold, Precious Metals, etc.
1613	Stationery, Greeting Cards, School Supplies
1906	Steam
1902	Telegraph
1901	Telephone
1624	Telephones, Telecommunications Equipment
1625	Textiles and Related Products
1629	Tile and Ceramic Merchandise
1203	Tires
1612	Tobacco Products
1632	Toys and Games
1210	Trailers
1214	Transmissions
1212	Trucks, Truck Parts
1109	Uniforms
1900	Utilities
1907	Water
1816	Well Drilling, Water Pumps
1811	Windows, Doors, Glass
1102	Women's & Girls' Clothing and/or Accessories

SERVICE BUSINESS CODES

Code	Description
2740	Accounting
2720	Advertising, Public Relations
2631	Aircraft and Related Supplies
2778	Alcoholic Beverage Pick-up & Transport
2775	Apartments, Condominiums, Homeowner Association
2100	Apparel
2404	Appliances, Housewares
2769	Appraising
2741	Architecture & Engineering Services
2717	Athletic Club (Spas, Gyms, etc.)
2405	Audio/Visual (TV, Stereo, Records, CD)
2217	Auto Body, Painting
2219	Auto Salvage/Junk Yard
2218	Auto Upholstery, Vinyl
2220	Auto Windows/Glass
2205	Automobiles
2200	Automotive
2705	Banks
2637	Bicycles & Related Merchandise
2213	Buses
2751	Cable TV
2614	Cameras, Photo Equipment & Supplies
2216	Car Wash & Wax
2767	Casino/Casino Hotel
2317	Catering
2764	Cemeteries, Crematories
2744	Charter Fishing

Code	Description
2711	Coin Operated Laundries
2602	Computer Hardware, Software
2754	Consulting Services (All Types)
2107	Custom Clothing & Tailoring
2761	Data Processing
2709	Dry Cleaning
2708	Duplicating, Photocopying
2903	Electric
2905	Electric and Gas
2630	Electronic Equipment
2779	Employer of Domestic/Household Employees
2745	Employment Agencies
2715	Entertainment (Amusement, Circus, Movies, & Sports)
2718	Equipment Rental/Leasing
2607	Farm & Garden Equipment & Supplies
2300	Food
2106	Footwear
2737	Funeral Services
2400	Furniture
2904	Gas
2204	Gasoline Service Station
2736	Governmental Services
2749	Graphics
2762	Hair Salons, Hair Dressers, Barber Shops
2752	Health Clubs/Programs (Exercise, Tanning, Diet)
2759	Hospitals, Clinics, Institutions
2701	Hotels & Motels
2768	Import/Export
2618	Industrial Tools & Equipment, Machinery
2755	Instructions (Dancing, Driving, etc.)
2732	Insurance
2729	Interior Cleaning/Janitorial, Rug Cleaning
2756	Interior Decorator
2742	Investment/Financial Services (Pension Plans)
2608	Jewelry
2725	Junk Dealers
2721	Landscaping, Lawn Service, Gardening
2617	Leather Goods and Luggage
2736	Linen Service & Rentals
2771	Locksmith
2728	Marinas, Boat & Dock Rentals, Bait
2730	Marine Maintenance & Repairs
2601	Medical Equipment
2600	Miscellaneous Products
2700	Miscellaneous Service
2753	Modeling Agencies
2621	Models & Hobby Related merchandise
2638	Monuments, Caskets & Related Merchandise
2201	Motor Vehicle Dealers (New and/or Used Autos)
2207	Motorboats
2209	Motorcycles, Minibikes
2215	Mufflers
2606	Musical Instruments & Related Merchandise
2719	Nursery, Day Care, Camps
2747	Nursing Homes & Convalescent Centers
2616	Optical Goods
2731	Organizations (Scouts, Fraternal, etc.)
2758	Parking/Parking Lots
2757	Participating Sports (Golf, Bowling, etc.)
2727	Pawn Brokers
2710	Pest Control
2723	Pet Grooming, Boarding, Training, Breeding
2707	Photo Printing & Processing
2706	Photographic, Sound Studios
2623	Pools & Related Accessories
2714	Printing and Publishing
2739	Professional Legal Services
2738	Professional Medical Services, Health Care
2704	Public Warehousing/Storage
2712	Radio and TV Repair

INSTRUCTIONS FOR
APPLICATION TO REGISTER A BUSINESS
IN NEW JERSEY
(CONTINUED)

TABLE A - NEW JERSEY BUSINESS CODES (continued)

Enter one of the following four-digit numbers in Block I to indicate the product group or service of your business:

Code	Description
2733	Real Estate
2202	Recreational Vehicles, Campers
2776	Recycling Related
2401	Refinishing, Upholstery, etc.
2702	Rooming & Boarding Houses
2748	Safe Deposit Boxes (Post Office, Bank)
2750	Security Services, Alarms
2773	Shipping & Mailing, Couriers
2620	Signs & Advertising Displays
2765	Snow Removal
2716	Social Club (Dating, etc.)
2605	Sporting Goods & Related Merchandise
2906	Steam
2770	Surveying
2902	Telegraph
2901	Telephone
2624	Telephones, Telecommunications Equipment
2203	Tires
2211	Towing
2632	Toys & Games
2703	Trailer Parks & Camps
2210	Trailers
2214	Transmissions
2734	Transportation (Limousines, Chauffeurs, Taxis, Buses)
2724	Trash Removal
2722	Travel Agencies
2743	Trucking and Moving
2212	Trucks
2763	Unions
2713	Upholstery & Furniture Repair, Refinishing
2900	Utilities
2774	Valet
2760	Veterinarians, Animal Hospitals
2772	Video Rentals & Related
2907	Water
2777	Water Systems Related (Purification, Pumps, etc.)
2766	Welding
2735	Window Washing
2746	Word Processing, Typing, Addressing, etc.

WHOLESALE BUSINESS CODES

Code	Description
3631	Aircraft & Relates Supplies
3314	Alcoholic Beverages/Liquor
3100	Apparel
3404	Appliances, Housewares, Linens
3622	Art, Mechanical Drawing & Related Supplies
3815	Asphalt
3405	Audio/Visual (TV, Stereo, Records, DC, etc.)
3208	Auto Parts & Related Products/Accessories
3220	Auto Windows/Glass
3200	Automotive
3306	Baked Goods
3637	Bicycles & Related Merchandise
3604	Books, Magazines, Periodicals, Newspapers
3316	Bottled Water
3809	Building Materials & Supplies
3800	Building/Construction
3213	Buses, Bus Parts
3614	Cameras, Photo Equipment & Supplies
3304	Candy, Nuts & Confectionery
3104	Children's & Infants' Clothing and/or Acces.
3602	Computer Hardware, Software
3808	Concrete
3627	Containers (Industrial/Commercial)
3110	Costumes
3305	Dairy Products
3601	Drugs & Medical Supplies, Medical Equipment
3502	Dry Goods
3903	Electric
3905	Electric & Gas
3804	Electrical Materials
3630	Electronic Equipment
3812	Energy Conservation Related

Code	Description
3105	Family Clothing
3607	Farm & Garden Equipment & Supplies
3823	Fencing
3611	Flowers & Related Merchandise
3300	Food
3106	Footwear
3103	Formal Wear (Tuxedos, Bridal Gowns, etc.)
3303	Fruit and/or Vegetables
3609	Fuel (Bottled Gas, Kerosene, Charcoal, etc.)
3400	Furniture
3108	Furriers
3904	Gas
3500	General Merchandise
3615	Gifts, Souvenirs
3301	Grocery Items
3634	Hair Grooming Supplies
3813	Hardware
3315	Health Food Products
3810	Heating, Ventilation & Air Conditioning
3401	Household Furniture & Furnishings
3610	Ice
3311	Ice Cream Products
3619	Industrial Supplies
3618	Industrial Tools & Equipment, Machinery
3820	Iron & Steel
3608	Jewelry
3406	Lamps, Lights, Shades
3617	Leather Goods & Luggage
3814	Lumber
3302	Meat and/or Fish
3101	Men's & Boys' Clothing and/or Accessories
3111	Millinery & Accessories
3626	Miscellaneous Decorative & Display Materials
3600	Miscellaneous Products
3621	Models & Hobby Related Merchandise
3638	Monuments, Caskets & Related Merchandise
3201	Motor Vehicles
3207	Motorboats
3209	Motorcycles, Minibikes
3215	Mufflers
3606	Musical Instruments & Related Merchandise
3318	Non-Alcoholic Beverages
3402	Office Furniture & Furnishings
3616	Optical Goods
3803	Paint, Wallpaper & Decorating
3633	Paintings, Sculpture & Related Artwork
3628	Paper & Packaging Products
3635	Perfumes & Cosmetics
3640	Pet Supplies
3313	Pizza
3802	Plumbing Materials
3623	Pools & Related Accessories
3202	Recreational Vehicles, Campers
3639	Religious Articles, Clothing & Related
3807	Roofing Materials
3403	Second Hand Items/Antiques
3822	Siding (Aluminum, Brickface, Stucco)
3620	Signs & Advertising Displays
3636	Soaps, Detergents, etc.
3307	Specialty Foods
3605	Sporting Goods & Related Merchandise
3603	Stamps, Coins, Gold, Precious Metals, etc.
3613	Stationery, Greeting Cards, School Supplies
3906	Steam
3902	Telegraph
3901	Telephone
3624	Telephones, Telecommunications Equipment
3625	Textiles & Related Products
3629	Tile & Ceramic Merchandise
3203	Tires
3612	Tobacco Products
3632	Toys & Games
3210	Trailers
3214	Transmissions
3212	Trucks, Truck Parts
3109	Uniforms

Code	Description
3900	Utilities
3907	Water
3816	Well Drilling, Water Pumps
3811	Windows, Doors, Glass
3102	Women's & Girls' Clothing and/or Accessories

CONSTRUCTION BUSINESS CODES

Code	Description
4815	Asphalt
4800	Building
4806	Carpentering & Wood Flooring
4808	Concrete Work
4817	Demolition, Excavation
4821	Dry Wall, Plaster
4804	Electrical Work
4812	Energy Conservation
4823	Fencing
4801	General Building Contractor
4810	Heating & Air Conditioning
4820	Iron & Steel
4805	Masonry & Stonework
4818	Miscellaneous Construction & Repair
4803	Painting, Paper Hanging & Decorating
4802	Plumbing
4807	Roofing
4819	Septic & Cesspool
4822	Siding (Aluminum, Brickface, Stucco)
4816	Well Drilling
4811	Windows, Doors, Glass

RETAIL BUSINESS CODES

Code	Description
5631	Aircraft & Related Supplies
5314	Alcoholic Beverages/Liquor
5508	Annual Shows
5100	Apparel
5404	Appliances, Housewares, Linens
5622	Art, Mechanical Drawing & Related Supplies
5815	Asphalt
5405	Audio/Visual (TV, Stereo, Records, CD, etc.)
5208	Auto Parts and Related Products/Accessories
5218	Auto Upholstery, Vinyl
5220	Auto Windows/Glass
5219	Automobile Junk/Scrap Yard
5206	Automobile Rentals and Leasing
5200	Automotive
5306	Bakeries
5309	Bars, Taverns, Pubs
5637	Bicycles and Related Merchandise
5604	Books, Magazines, Periodicals, Newspapers
5316	Bottled Water
5800	Building
5809	Building Materials and Supplies
5213	Buses, Bus Parts
5614	Cameras, Photo Equipment and Supplies
5304	Candy, Nuts and Confectionery
5317	Catering
5104	Children's & Infants' Clothing and/or Accessories
5641	Collectors Items (Baseball Cards, Comics, etc.)
5602	Computer Hardware, Software
5808	Concrete
5627	Containers (Industrial/Commercial)
5110	Costumes
5107	Custom Clothing and Tailoring
5305	Dairy Products
5501	Department Store
5506	Direct Selling Organization (Amway, etc.)
5601	Drugs and Medical Supplies, Medical Equipment
5502	Dry Goods and General Merchandise
5804	Electrical Materials
5630	Electronic Equipment
5812	Energy Conservation Related
5105	Family Clothing
5607	Farm and Garden Equipment and Supplies

INSTRUCTIONS FOR
APPLICATION TO REGISTER A BUSINESS
IN NEW JERSEY
(CONTINUED)

Code	Description	Code	Description	Code	Description
5312	Fast Food (Burgers, Chicken, Hot Dogs, Tacos, etc.)	5504	Limited Price Variety Store	5202	Recreational Vehicles, Campers
5823	Fencing	5814	Lumber	5639	Religious Articles, Clothing and Related
5507	Flea Markets	5503	Mail Order House	5310	Restaurants (With Liquor)
5611	Flowers and Related Merchandise	5302	Meat and Fish	5308	Restaurants, Diners, Eateries (No Liquor)
5300	Food	5101	Men's and Boy's Clothing and/or Accessories	5807	Roofing Materials
5106	Footwear	5505	Merchandise Vending Machine Operator	5403	Second Hand Items/Antiques
5103	Formal Wear (Tuxedos, Bridal Gowns)	5111	Millinery and Accessories	5822	Siding
5303	Fruit and Vegetables, Produce Stands	5626	Miscellaneous Decorative & Display Materials	5620	Signs and Advertising Displays
5609	Fuel (Bottled Gas, Kerosene, Charcoal, etc.)	5600	Miscellaneous Products	5636	Soaps, Detergents, etc.
5400	Furniture	5621	Models and Hobby Related Merchandise	5307	Specialty Foods (Charles Chips)
5108	Furriers	5638	Monuments, Caskets & Related Merchandise	5605	Sporting Goods and Related Merchandise
5500	General Merchandise	5201	Motor Vehicle Dealers (New and /or Used Autos)	5603	Stamps, Coins, Gold, Precious Metals, etc.
5615	Gifts, Souvenirs			5613	Stationery, Greeting Cards, School Supplies
5301	Groceries Including Delicatessens	5207	Motorboats	5624	Telephones, Telecommunications Equipment
5634	Hair Grooming Supplies	5209	Motorcycles, Minibikes	5625	Textiles and Related Products
5813	Hardware	5215	Mufflers	5629	Tile and Ceramic Merchandise
5315	Health Foods	5606	Musical Instruments and Related Merchandise	5203	Tires
5810	Heating, Ventilation & Air Conditioning	5318	Non-Alcoholic Beverages	5612	Tobacco Products
5401	Household Furniture & Furnishings	5402	Office Furniture, Equipment and Supplies	5632	Toys and Games
5610	Ice	5616	Optical Goods	5210	Trailers
5311	Ice Cream Products	5803	Paint, Wallpaper	5214	Transmissions
5619	Industrial Supplies	5633	Paintings, Sculpture and Related Artwork	5212	Trucks, Truck Parts
5618	Industrial Tools and Equipment, Machinery	5628	Paper and Packaging Products	5109	Uniforms
5820	Iron and Steel	5635	Perfumes and Cosmetics	5816	Well Drilling, Water Pumps
5608	Jewelry	5640	Pet Supplies	5811	Windows, Doors, Glass
5406	Lamps, Lights, Shades	5313	Pizzerias	5102	Women's and Girl's Clothing and/or Accessories
5617	Leather Goods and Luggage	5802	Plumbing Materials		
		5623	Pools and Related Accessories		

INSTRUCTIONS FOR
APPLICATION TO REGISTER A BUSINESS
IN NEW JERSEY
(CONTINUED)

Location Code	Municipality	Location Code	Municipality	Location Code	Municipality	Location Code	Municipality
ATLANTIC COUNTY		0258	Saddle River Bor.	0427	Pennsauken Twp.	0813	Newfield Bor.
0101	Absecon City	0259	South Hackensack Twp.	0428	Pine Hill Bor.	0814	Paulsboro Bor.
0102	Atlantic City	0260	Teaneck Twp.	0429	Pine Valley Bor.	0815	Pitman Bor.
0103	Brigantine City	0261	Tenafly Bor.	0430	Runnemede Bor.	0816	South Harrison Twp.
0104	Buena Bor.	0262	Teterboro Bor.	0431	Somerdale Bor.	0817	Swedesboro Bor.
0105	Buena Vista Twp.	0263	Upper Saddle River Bor.	0432	Stratford Bor.	0818	Washington Twp.
0106	Corbin City City	0264	Waldwick Bor.	0433	Tavistock Bor.	0819	Wenonah Bor.
0107	Egg Harbor City	0265	Wallington Bor.	0434	Voorhees Twp.	0820	West Deptford Twp.
0108	Egg Harbor Twp.	0266	Washington Twp.	0435	Waterford Twp.	0821	Westville Bor.
0109	Estell Manor City	0267	Westwood Bor.	0436	Winslow Twp.	0822	Woodbury City
0110	Folsom Bor.	0268	Woodcliff Lake Bor.	0437	Woodlynne Bor.	0823	Woodbury Heights Bor.
0111	Galloway Twp.	0269	Wood-Ridge Bor.			0824	Woolwich Twp.
0112	Hamilton Twp.	0270	Wyckoff Twp.	**CAPE MAY COUNTY**			
0113	Hammonton Town			0501	Avalon Bor.	**HUDSON COUNTY**	
0114	Linwood City	**BURLINGTON COUNTY**		0502	Cape May City	0901	Bayonne City
0115	Longport Bor.	0301	Bass River Twp.	0503	Cape May Point Bor.	0902	East Newark Bor.
0116	Margate City	0302	Beverly City	0504	Dennis Twp.	0903	Guttenberg Town
0117	Mullica Twp.	0303	Bordentown City	0505	Lower Twp.	0904	Harrison Town
0118	Northfield City	0304	Bordentown Twp.	0506	Middle Twp.	0905	Hoboken City
0119	Pleasantville City	0305	Burlington City	0507	North Wildwood City	0906	Jersey City City
0120	Port Republic City	0306	Burlington Twp.	0508	Ocean City City	0907	Kearny Town
0121	Somers Point City	0307	Chesterfield Twp.	0509	Sea Isle City City	0908	North Bergen Twp.
0122	Ventnor City	0308	Cinnaminson Twp.	0510	Stone Harbor Bor.	0909	Secaucus Town
0123	Weymouth Twp.	0309	Delanco Twp.	0511	Upper Twp.	0910	Union City City
		0310	Delran Twp.	0512	West Cape May Bor.	0911	Weehawken Twp.
BERGEN COUNTY		0311	Eastampton Twp.	0513	West Wildwood Bor.	0912	West New York
0201	Allendale Bor.	0312	Edgewater Park Twp.	0514	Wildwood City		
0202	Alpine Bor.	0313	Evesham Twp.	0515	Wildwood Crest Bor.	**HUNTERDON COUNTY**	
0203	Bergenfield Bor.	0314	Fieldsboro Bor.	0516	Woodbine Bor.	1001	Alexandria Twp.
0204	Bogota Bor.	0315	Florence Twp.			1002	Bethlehem Twp.
0205	Carlstadt Bor.	0316	Hainesport Twp.	**CUMBERLAND COUNTY**		1003	Bloomsbury Bor.
0206	Cliffside Park Bor.	0317	Lumberton Twp.	0601	Bridgeton City	1004	Califon Bor.
0207	Closter Bor.	0318	Mansfield Twp.	0602	Commercial City	1005	Clinton Town
0208	Cresskill Bor.	0319	Maple Shade Twp.	0603	Deerfield Twp.	1006	Clinton Twp.
0209	Demarest Bor.	0320	Medford Twp.	0604	Downe Twp.	1007	Delaware Twp.
0210	Dumont Bor.	0321	Medford Lakes Bor.	0605	Fairfield Twp.	1008	East Amwell Twp.
0211	Elmwood Park Bor.	0322	Moorestown Twp.	0606	Greenwich Twp.	1009	Flemington Bor.
0212	East Rutherford Bor.	0323	Mount Holly Twp.	0607	Hopewell Twp.	1010	Franklin Twp.
0213	Edgewater Bor.	0324	Mount Laurel Twp.	0608	Lawrence Twp.	1011	Frenchtown Bor.
0214	Emerson Bor.	0325	New Hanover Twp.	0609	Maurice River Twp.	1012	Glen Gardner Bor.
0215	Englewood City	0326	No. Hanover Twp.	0610	Millville City	1013	Hampton Bor.
0216	Englewood Cliffs Bor.	0327	Palmyra Bor.	0611	Shiloh Bor.	1014	High Bridge Bor.
0217	Fair Lawn Bor.	0328	Pemberton Bor.	0612	Stow Creek Twp.	1015	Holland Twp.
0218	Fairview Bor.	0329	Pemberton Twp.	0613	Upper Deerfield Twp.	1016	Kingswood Twp.
0219	Fort Lee Bor.	0330	Riverside Twp.	0614	Vineland City	1017	Lambertville City
0220	Franklin Lakes Bor.	0331	Riverton Bor.			1018	Lebanon Bor.
0221	Garfield City	0332	Shamong Twp.	**ESSEX COUNTY**		1019	Lebanon Twp.
0222	Glen Rock Bor.	0333	Southampton Twp.	0701	Belleville Twp.	1020	Milford Bor.
0223	Hackensack City	0334	Springfield Twp.	0702	Bloomfield Twp.	1021	Raritan Twp.
0224	Harrington Park Bor.	0335	Tabernacle Twp.	0703	Caldwell Borough Twp.	1022	Readington Twp.
0225	Hasbrouck Heights Bor.	0336	Washington Twp.	0704	Cedar Grove Twp.	1023	Stockton Bor.
0226	Haworth Bor.	0337	Westampton Twp.	0705	East Orange City	1024	Tewksbury Twp.
0227	Hillsdale Bor.	0338	Willingboro Twp.	0706	Essex Fells Twp.	1025	Union Twp.
0228	Hohokus Bor.	0339	Woodland Twp.	0707	Fairfield Twp.	1026	West Amwell Twp.
0229	Leonia Bor.	0340	Wrightstown Bor.	0708	Glen Ridge Twp.		
0230	Little Ferry Bor.			0709	Irvington Twp.	**MERCER COUNTY**	
0231	Lodi Bor.	**CAMDEN COUNTY**		0710	Livingston Twp.	1101	East Windsor Twp.
0232	Lyndhurst Twp.	0401	Audubon Bor.	0711	Maplewood Twp.	1102	Ewing Twp.
0233	Mahwah Twp.	0402	Audubon Park Bor.	0712	Millburn Twp.	1103	Hamilton Twp.
0234	Maywood Bor.	0403	Barrington Bor.	0713	Montclair Twp.	1104	Hightstown Bor.
0235	Midland Park Bor.	0404	Bellmawr Bor.	0714	Newark City	1105	Hopewell Bor.
0236	Montvale Bor.	0405	Berlin Bor.	0715	North Caldwell Twp.	1106	Hopewell Twp.
0237	Moonachie Bor.	0406	Berlin Twp.	0716	Nutley Twp.	1107	Lawrence Twp.
0238	New Milford Bor.	0407	Brooklawn Bor.	0717	Orange City Twp.	1108	Pennington Bor.
0239	North Arlington Bor.	0408	Camden City	0718	Roseland Bor.	1109	Princeton Bor.
0240	Northvale Bor.	0409	Cherry Hill Twp.	0719	South Orange Village	1110	Princeton Twp.
0241	Norwood Bor.	0410	Chesilhurst Bor.	0720	Verona Twp.	1111	Trenton City
0242	Oakland Bor.	0411	Clementon Bor.	0721	West Caldwell Twp.	1112	Washington Twp.
0243	Old Tappan Bor.	0412	Collingswood Bor.	0722	West Orange Twp.	1113	West Windsor Twp.
0244	Oradell Bor.	0413	Gibbsboro Bor.				
0245	Palisades Park Bor.	0414	Gloucester City	**GLOUCESTER COUNTY**		**MIDDLESEX COUNTY**	
0246	Paramus Bor.	0415	Gloucester Twp.	0801	Clayton Bor.	1201	Carteret Bor.
0247	Park Ridge Bor.	0416	Haddon Twp.	0802	Deptford Twp.	1202	Cranbury Twp.
0248	Ramsey Bor.	0417	Haddonfield Bor.	0803	East Greenwich Twp.	1203	Dunellen Bor.
0249	Ridgefield Bor.	0418	Haddon Heights Bor.	0804	Elk Twp.	1204	East Brunswick Twp.
0250	Ridgefield Park Village	0419	Hi Nella Bor.	0805	Franklin Twp.	1205	Edison Twp.
0251	Ridgewood Village	0420	Laurel Springs Bor.	0806	Glassboro Bor.	1206	Helmetta Bor.
0252	Riveredge Bor.	0421	Lawnside Bor.	0807	Greenwich Twp.	1207	Highland Park Bor.
0253	Rivervale Twp.	0422	Lindenwold Bor.	0808	Harrison Twp.	1208	Jamesburg Bor.
0254	Rochelle Park Twp.	0423	Magnolia Bor.	0809	Logan Twp.	1209	Metuchen Bor.
0255	Rockleigh Bor.	0424	Merchantville Bor.	0810	Mantua Twp.	1210	Middlesex Bor.
0256	Rutherford Bor.	0425	Mt. Ephraim Bor.	0811	Monroe Twp.	1211	Milltown Bor.
0257	Saddle Brook Twp.	0426	Oaklyn Bor.	0812	National Park Bor.	1212	Monroe Twp.

- 12 -

INSTRUCTIONS FOR
APPLICATION TO REGISTER A BUSINESS
IN NEW JERSEY
(CONTINUED)

TABLE B - NEW JERSEY COUNTY / MUNICIPALITY CODES

Enter the Appropriate Four-Digit Number in the Boxes Provided on Page 17, Item J.

Location Code	Municipality
1213	New Brunswick City
1214	North Brunswick Twp.
1215	Old Bridge Twp.
1216	Perth Amboy City
1217	Piscataway Twp.
1218	Plainsboro Twp.
1219	Sayreville Bor.
1220	South Amboy City
1221	South Brunswick Twp.
1222	South Plainfield Bor.
1223	South River Bor.
1224	Spotswood Bor.
1225	Woodbridge Twp.

MONMOUTH COUNTY

Location Code	Municipality
1301	Aberdeen Twp.
1302	Allenhurst Bor.
1303	Allentown Bor.
1304	Asbury Park City
1305	Atlantic Highlands Bor.
1306	Avon-by-the-sea Bor.
1307	Belmar Bor.
1308	Bradley Beach Bor.
1309	Brielle Bor.
1310	Colts Neck Twp.
1311	Deal Bor.
1312	Eatontown Bor.
1313	Englishtown Bor.
1314	Fair Haven Bor.
1315	Farmingdale
1316	Freehold Bor.
1317	Freehold Twp.
1318	Hazlet Twp.
1319	Highlands Bor.
1320	Holmdel Twp.
1321	Howell Twp.
1322	Interlaken Bor.
1323	Keansburg Bor.
1324	Keyport Bor.
1325	Little Silver Bor.
1326	Loch Arbour Village
1327	Long Branch City
1328	Manalapan Twp.
1329	Manasquan Bor.
1330	Marlboro Twp.
1331	Matawan Bor.
1332	Middletown Twp.
1333	Millstone Twp.
1334	Monmouth Beach Bor.
1335	Neptune Twp.
1336	Neptune City Bor.
1337	Ocean Twp.
1338	Oceanport Bor.
1339	Red Bank Bor.
1340	Roosevelt Bor.
1341	Rumson Bor.
1342	Sea Bright Bor.
1343	Sea Girt Bor.
1344	Shrewsbury Bor.
1345	Shrewsbury Twp.
1346	South Belmar Bor.
1347	Spring Lake Bor.
1348	Spring Lake Heights Bor.
1349	Tinton Falls Bor.
1350	Union Beach Bor.
1351	Upper Freehold Twp.
1352	Wall Twp.
1353	West Long Branch Bor.

MORRIS COUNTY

Location Code	Municipality
1401	Boonton Town
1402	Boonton Twp.
1403	Butler Bor.
1404	Chatham Bor.
1405	Chatham Twp.
1406	Chester Bor.
1407	Chester Twp.
1408	Denville Twp.
1409	Dover Twp.
1410	East Hanover Twp.
1411	Florham Park Bor.
1312	Hanover Twp.
1413	Harding Twp.
1414	Jefferson Twp.
1415	Kinnelon Bor.
1416	Lincoln Park Bor.
1417	Madison Bor.
1418	Mendham Bor.
1419	Mendham Twp.
1420	Mine Hill Twp.
1421	Montville Twp.
1422	Morris Twp.
1423	Morris Plains Bor.
1424	Morristown Town
1425	Mountain Lakes Bor.
1426	Mount Arlington Bor.
1427	Mount Olive Twp.
1428	Netcong Bor.
1429	Par-Troy Hills Twp.
1430	Passaic Twp.
1431	Pequannock Twp.
1432	Randolph Twp.
1433	Riverdale Bor.
1434	Rockaway Bor.
1435	Rockaway Twp.
1436	Roxbury Twp.
1437	Victory Gardens Bor.
1438	Washington Twp.
1439	Wharton Bor.

OCEAN COUNTY

Location Code	Municipality
1501	Barnegat Twp.
1502	Barnegat Light Bor.
1503	Bay Head Bor.
1504	Beach Haven Bor.
1505	Beachwood Bor.
1506	Berkeley Twp.
1507	Brick Twp.
1508	Dover Twp.
1509	Eaglewood Twp.
1510	Harvey Cedars Bor.
1511	Island Heights Bor.
1512	Jackson Twp.
1513	Lacey Twp.
1514	Lakehurst Bor.
1515	Lakewood Twp.
1516	Lavallette Bor.
1517	Little Egg Harbor Twp.
1518	Long Beach Twp.
1519	Manchester Twp.
1520	Mantoloking Bor.
1521	Ocean Twp.
1522	Ocean Gate Bor.
1523	Pine Beach Bor.
1524	Plumsted Twp.
1525	Pt. Pleasant Bor.
1526	Pt. Pleasant Beach Bor.
1527	Seaside Heights Bor.
1528	Seaside Park Bor.
1529	Ship Bottom Bor.
1530	South Toms River Bor.
1531	Stafford Twp.
1532	Surf City Bor.
1533	Tuckerton Bor.

PASSAIC COUNTY

Location Code	Municipality
1601	Bloomingdale Bor.
1602	Clifton City
1603	Haledon Bor.
1604	Hawthorne Bor.
1605	Little Falls Twp.
1606	North Haledon Bor.
1607	Passaic City
1608	Paterson City
1609	Pompton Lakes Bor.
1610	Prospect Park Bor.
1611	Ringwood Bor.
1612	Totowa Bor.
1613	Wanaque Bor.
1614	Wayne Twp.
1615	West Milford Twp.
1616	West Paterson Bor.

SALEM COUNTY

Location Code	Municipality
1701	Alloway Twp.
1702	Carneys Point Twp.
1703	Elmer Bor.
1704	Elsinboro Twp.
1705	Lower Alloways Creek Twp.
1706	Mannington Twp.
1707	Oldmans Twp.
1708	Penns Grove Bor.
1709	Pennsville Twp.
1710	Pilesgrove Twp.
1711	Pittsgrove Twp.
1712	Quinton Twp.
1713	Salem City
1714	Upper Pittsgrove Twp.
1715	Woodstown Bor

SOMERSET COUNTY

Location Code	Municipality
1801	Bedminster Twp.
1802	Bernards Twp.
1803	Bernardsville Bor.
1804	Bound Brook Bor.
1805	Branchburg Twp.
1806	Bridgewater Twp.
1807	Far Hills Bor.
1808	Franklin Twp.
1809	Green Brook Twp.
1810	Hillsborough Twp.
1811	Manville Bor.
1812	Millstone Bor.
1813	Montgomery Twp.
1814	North Plainfield Bor.
1815	Peapack-Gladstone Bor.
1816	Raritan Twp.
1817	Rocky Hill Bor.
1818	Somerville Bor.
1819	South Bound Brook Bor.
1820	Warren Twp.
1821	Watchung Bor.

SUSSEX COUNTY

Location Code	Municipality
1901	Andover Bor.
1902	Andover Twp.
1903	Branchville Bor.
1904	Byram Twp.
1905	Frankford Twp.
1906	Franklin Bor.
1907	Fredon Twp.
1908	Green Twp.
1909	Hamburg Bor.
1910	Hampton Twp.
1911	Hardystown Twp.
1912	Hopatcong Bor.
1913	Lafayette Twp.
1914	Montague Twp.
1915	Newton Town
1916	Ogdensburg Bor.
1917	Sandyston Twp.
1918	Sparta Twp.
1919	Stanhope Bor.
1920	Stillwater Twp.
1921	Sussex Bor.
1922	Vernon Twp.
1923	Walpack Twp.
1924	Wantage Twp.

UNION COUNTY

Location Code	Municipality
2001	Berkleley Heights Twp.
2002	Clark Twp.
2003	Cranford Twp.
2004	Elizabeth City
2005	Fanwood Bor.
2006	Garwood Bor.
2007	Hillside Twp.
2008	Kenilworth Bor.
2009	Linden City
2010	Mountainside Bor.
2011	New Providence Bor.
2012	Plainfield City
2013	Rahway City
2014	Roselle Bor.
2015	Roselle Park Bor.
2016	Scotch Plains
2017	Springfield Twp.
2018	Summit City
2019	Union Twp.
2020	Westfield Town
2021	Winfield Twp.

WARREN COUNTY

Location Code	Municipality
2101	Allamuchy Twp.
2102	Alpha Bor.
2103	Belvidere Town
2104	Blairstown Twp.
2105	Franklin Twp.
2106	Frelinghuysen Twp.
2107	Greenwich Twp.
2108	Hackettstown Town
2109	Hardwick Twp.
2110	Harmony Twp.
2111	Hope Twp.
2112	Independence Twp.
2113	Knowlton Twp.
2114	Liberty Twp.
2115	Lopatcong Twp.
2116	Mansfield Twp.
2117	Oxford Twp.
2118	Pahaquarry Twp.
2119	Phillipsburg Town
2120	Pohatcong Twp.
2121	Washington Bor.
2122	Washington Twp.
2123	White Twp.

Location Code	Municipality
2200	ALABAMA
2300	ALASKA
2400	ARIZONA
2500	ARKANSAS
2600	CALIFORNIA
2700	COLORADO
2800	CONNECTICUT
2900	DELAWARE
3000	DISTRICT OF COLUMBIA
3100	FLORIDA
3200	GEORGIA
3300	HAWAII
3400	IDAHO
3500	ILLINOIS
3600	INDIANA
3700	IOWA
3800	KANSAS
3900	KENTUCKY
4000	LOUISIANA
4100	MAINE
4200	MARYLAND
4300	MASSACHUSETTS
4400	MICHIGAN
4500	MINNESOTA
4600	MISSISSIPPI
4700	MISSOURI
4800	MONTANA
4900	NEBRASKA
5000	NEVADA
5100	NEW HAMPSHIRE
5300	NEW MEXICO
5400	NEW YORK
5500	NORTH CAROLINA
5600	NORTH DAKOTA
5700	OHIO
5800	OKLAHOMA
5900	OREGON
6000	PENNSYLVANIA
6100	RHODE ISLAND
6200	SOUTH CAROLINA
6300	SOUTH DAKOTA
6400	TENNESSEE
6500	TEXAS
6600	UTAH
6700	VERMONT
6800	VIRGINIA
6900	WASHINGTON
7000	WEST VIRGINIA
7100	WISCONSIN
7200	WYOMING
7300	PUERTO RICO
7400	NETHERLANDS
7500	BELGIUM
7600	ARGENTINA
7700	CANADA
7800	MEXICO
7900	VIRGIN ISLANDS
8000	ENGLAND
8100	CHINA
8200	GERMANY
8300	IRELAND
8400	GREECE
8500	ISRAEL

INSTRUCTIONS FOR
APPLICATION TO REGISTER A BUSINESS
IN NEW JERSEY
(CONTINUED)

DIVISION OF TAXATION
District Offices

Offices for Taxpayers Assistance and Forms

TRENTON — Taxation Building
50 Barrack St. — 1st Floor Lobby
Box CN 269
Trenton, NJ 08646
(609) 292-6400
Toll Free: (800) 323-4400

REGIONAL OFFICES:

ASBURY PARK

630 Bangs Avenue
Asbury Park, NJ 07712
(732) 869-8044

CAMDEN

One Port Center, Suite 200
Camden, NJ 08103

FAIR LAWN

2208 Route 208, South
Fair Lawn, NJ 07410
(201) 791-0500

NEWARK

124 Halsey Street, 2nd Floor
Newark, NJ 07101
(973) 648-2567

NORTHFIELD

1915-A New Road, Rt. 9
Northfield, NJ 08225
(609) 645-6673

QUAKERBRIDGE

NO WALK-IN ASSISTANCE
Conference and Appeals Branch
Quakerbridge Plaza Office Complex
Bldg. 5 - 3rd Floor Quakerbridge
Mercerville, NJ 08619

SOMERVILLE

75 Veterans Memorial Dr. East
Suite 103
Somerville, NJ 08876

You may also register your business online by going to the NJ web site at:
http://www.state.nj.us/treasury/revenue/dcr/reg/sos_dcrnew01.prod.htm

Hours of operation 8:30 a.m. to 4:30 p.m. Monday through Friday.

NEW JERSEY WEB SITE

WWW.STATE.NJ.US/NJBIZ/

NEW JERSEY HOTLINES

Personal Income Tax . . . . .(609) 633-6657
Business Tax . . . .(609) 633-6900

7

RECORD KEEPING FOR THE NEW JERSEY SALES TAX BUREAU

In a prior chapter we discussed the type of bookkeeping system you might maintain for your business. If you adhere to these suggestions, save all your receipts, and report your income/expenses properly, you'll be in good shape for most IRS audits. Unfortunately, the State of New Jersey Sales Tax Bureau conducts a different type of audit. They are interested in your payment of sales tax. The State of New Jersey may also conduct an audit of income and expenses in addition to the audit for sales tax.

In New Jersey, many items are subject to the 7% sales tax. This means that you as a business owner would collect the sales tax and every month or quarter remit what you have collected to the New Jersey Sales Tax Bureau.

If you sell taxable items or provide taxable services in New Jersey, you are required to collect 7% sales tax and remit it to the State. You must file a New Jersey Sales and Use Tax Quarterly Return ST-50 every three months, even if in that particular quarter you collected no tax. Businesses that collect more than $500 per month in sales tax must also file the monthly remittance statements ST-51. As of January 1, 2005, all sales tax submissions must be made on-line or by phone.

What actually happens in a sales tax audit is that the State requires the business to prove why they did not send in sales tax on certain items. As an example, many retailers and wholesalers sell taxable and non-taxable items. When the business owner submits his quarterly sales tax form, he shows the taxable and non-taxable sales. The State may actually come in and ask you to prove why you did not collect and remit sales tax on certain goods.

The on-line quarterly sales tax form is shown on the following page with the State's instructions for filing.

NJ Division of Taxation
Sales and Use Tax Quarterly Return
Confirmation

ST-50

FEIN: 222-   **Quarter/Yr: 4/2006**

Business Name: JAMY'S DONUT SHOPPE

Quarter Ending Date: 12/31/2006   **Return Due Date: 01/20/2007**
Date Filed: 01/06/2007

This screen enables you to review information that you have entered. It is for your use only. Please do not mail this page to the Division.

Thank you for using our online service. Following is your filing confirmation. If you made a payment with your filing, the confirmation number also serves as your payment confirmation.

Your Return Has Been Submitted To The Division.

Please note that receipt of a confirmation number means that the return has been submitted for processing, and your authority given to collect the payment amount from your financial institution. Please check with your bank to verify that the payment was made.

```
Confirmation Number: 55-11849
Bank Routing Number: *****1935
Account Number: *****9386
Type: Checking
Payment Method: Electronic Check
Settlement Date: 01/07/2007
Payment Amount: $370.00
Total WEB Payments: $370.00
```

1. Gross Receipts for Quarter (To Nearest Dollar)	$ 18500.00
2. Deductions (To Nearest Dollar)	$ 6071.00
3. Balance Subject to Tax (Line 1 minus Line 2)	$ 12429.00
4. Sales Tax Due (Greater of amount collected or applicable rate of Line 3)	$ 870.00
5. Use Tax Due	$ 0.00
6. Total Tax Due (Line 4 plus Line 5)	$ 870.00
7. Total Monthly Payments	$ 500.00
8. Quarterly Amount Due (Line 6 minus Line 7)	$ 370.00
9. Penalty and Interest	$ 0.00
10. Adjusted Amount Due (Line 8 plus Line 9)	$ 370.00

To make an additional payment, select a payment method and press "Make Additional Payment".   Electronic Check

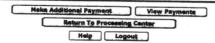

We are very interested in your comments regarding this new online inquiry. Contact the Division via at E-MAIL taxation@tax.state.nj.us to submit your comments.

N.J. QUARTERLY ON-LINE REPORTING FORM

New Jersey Sales and Use Tax EZ TeleFile System

(Forms ST-51 Monthly Return and ST-50 Quarterly Return)

Instructions

Filing Forms ST-50/51 by Phone

Complete the EZ TeleFile Worksheet, call the Business Paperless Telefiling System at 1-877-829-2866, and select "1" from the menu for the Sales and Use Tax EZ File System. You will be prompted to enter the information from your worksheet on your Touch-tone telephone keypad. (NOTE: For best results, do not use a cordless or cellular phone or one with a keypad in the handset.) The system provides step-by-step instructions and repeats your entries to ensure accuracy. When your return is accepted, you will be given a 7-digit Confirmation Number as proof that your return was successfully filed. The telefiling system is available 24 hours a day, seven days a week.

Payments. The system automatically calculates the total amount due. You will have an opportunity to pay the amount due by electronic check (e-check) during your phone call. Enter your bank information on your worksheet if you want to pay by e-check. You can also pay your liability by credit card or electronic funds transfer (EFT). Payments must be made electronically using one of these methods. See "How to Pay," below.

Identification. You will be asked to enter your New Jersey Taxpayer Identification Number and either your 4-digit sales tax Personal Identification Number (PIN) or the first four characters of your registered taxpayer name to access the system.

Filing Online

You can also file your Sales and Use Tax Returns (Forms ST-50/51) online at the Division of Taxation's Web site (www.state.nj.us/treasury/taxation/). Choose "File Online" on the navigation bar, scroll down to "Sales and Use Tax," select "Form ST-50/51," and follow the filing instructions.

Other Sales and Use Tax Returns

The forms listed below cannot be filed through the S&U EZ File System. Taxpayers must continue to complete and file these forms on paper according to the instructions that accompany the forms.

- Combined Atlantic City Luxury Tax/State Sales Tax (Form ST-250).
- Cape May County Tourism Sales Tax (Form ST-350).
- Sales and Use Tax - Salem County (Form ST-450/451).
- Combined State Sales and Use Tax/Urban Enterprise Zone Sales Tax (Form UZ-50).
- NJ/NY Combined State Sales and Use Tax (Form ST-20/ST-21).
- Annual Business Use Tax Return (Form ST-18B).
- Sales and Use Tax Energy Return (Form ST-EN).

Who Must File

Every entity registered in New Jersey to collect sales tax or to remit use tax must file sales and use tax returns on a regular basis. The amount of tax due for each filing period must be remitted to the State on or before the due date of the return.

All businesses are required to file a quarterly return (Form ST-50) for each quarter even if no tax is due and/or no sales were made for that particular quarter. The quarterly return must show total gross receipts for the entire three-month period covered by that quarterly return. Receipts from lease transactions are *not* to be included in gross receipts for the quarter. A monthly return (Form ST-51) must also be filed for the first and/or second month of a calendar quarter if the amount of tax due for that month exceeds $500. Taxpayers that are registered to remit payments by electronic funds transfer (EFT) must make monthly payments of sales and use tax as required and must file ST-50 quarterly returns. EFT payers are not required to file ST-51 monthly returns.

This packet contains four EZ TeleFile Worksheets — one for each calendar quarter. You will record both your monthly (if required) and quarterly return information on the same worksheet. The EZ TeleFile Worksheets may be reproduced for future use. Copies are also available online or by phone. See "Where to Get Information" on page 4.

When to File

Both monthly and quarterly returns are due by the 20th day of the month following the period covered by the return. For example, a monthly return (Form ST-51) for the month of November must be filed no later than December 20 and a quarterly return (Form ST-50) for the fourth quarter (ending December 31) must be filed by January 20. If a due date falls on a Saturday, Sunday, or legal holiday, the return is due on the next business day. Returns transmitted by 11:59 p.m. on the due date will be deemed timely.

How to Pay

Payments made by e-check or credit card by 11:59 p.m. on the due date will be deemed timely even if the settlement date (date payment is debited from the account) is the next business day.

Electronic Check (e-check)
You will be given an opportunity during your telephone call to pay your tax liability by e-check. If you choose to pay by e-check, be sure to enter the 9-digit routing number and the account number (up to 17 characters – numbers only) in the Payment Information section of the worksheet **before** you make your call.

If you choose not to pay the tax due when you file your return, you can make an e-check payment by itself in a separate call later. However, your payment must be made by the due date to avoid penalty and interest charges.

Credit Card
To pay your tax liability by credit card, call 1-800-2PAYTAX, toll-free or go to www.officialpayments.com after you have completed your telephone filing and received a Confirmation

SALES AND USE TAX INSTRUCTIONS

Number. There is a convenience fee of 2.5% of your liability paid directly to Official Payments Corporation.

Electronic Funds Transfer (EFT)
Taxpayers with a prior year liability of $10,000 or more in any tax are required to make their payments for all taxes by EFT. Other taxpayers may voluntarily submit payments by EFT with the approval of the Division of Revenue. EFT payments are separate transactions made outside the Business Paperless Telefiling System. For more information on the EFT Program, call 609-984-9830, write to New Jersey Division of Revenue, EFT Unit, PO Box 191, Trenton, NJ 08646-0191, or visit the Division of Revenue's Web site at www.state.nj.us/treasury/revenue/.

Penalties, Interest, and Fees
Failure to file a return by the due date and/or failure to remit any taxes due by the due date will result in penalty and interest charges. Anyone required to collect sales and use tax does so as a trustee on behalf of the State of New Jersey. Thus, business owners, partners, corporate officers, and some employees of such businesses may be held personally liable for failure to collect the tax when required or for failure to file returns and remit any taxes due on a timely basis.

Late Filing Penalties
5% per month (or fraction thereof) of the balance of tax liability due at original return due date not to exceed 25% of such tax liability. A penalty of $100 per month (or fraction thereof) for each month the return is late will also be imposed.

Late Payment Penalty
5% of the balance of the taxes due and paid late.

Interest
The annual interest rate is 3% above the average predominant prime rate. Interest is imposed each month (or fraction thereof) on the unpaid balance of the tax from the original due date to the date of payment. At the end of each calendar year any tax, penalties, and interest remaining due will become part of the balance on which interest is charged.

NOTE: The average predominant prime rate is the rate as determined by the Board of Governors of the Federal Reserve System, quoted by commercial banks to large businesses on December 1st of the calendar year immediately preceding the calendar year in which the payment was due or as determined by the Director in accordance with N.J.S.A. 54:48-2.

Collection Fees
In addition to the above penalties and interest, if your tax bill is sent to a collection agency, a referral cost recovery fee of 10% of the tax due will be added to your liability. If a certificate of debt is issued for your outstanding liability, a fee for the cost of collection may also be imposed.

General Information
Lease Transactions
Lessors are responsible for paying use tax on property that is leased. The total amount of tax due from the lessor must be paid on or before the 20th day of the month immediately following the lease transaction. The amount of use tax being remitted must be included on Line 2 of the monthly return (Form ST-51) and Line 6 of the quarterly return (Form ST-50).

Gross Receipts
The accrual method of accounting must be used when reporting gross receipts. Under this method, all receipts are re-

ported in the period in which the sale took place, no matter when, or if, payment is actually received from the customer.

Report gross receipts from all transactions, *including exempt transactions,* which occurred during the three-month reporting period covered by the quarterly return (Form ST-50). This includes, but is not limited to:

- Sales of tangible personal property, including the rental, storage, and use of tangible personal property.
- Sales of services.
- Sales of prepared foods.
- Room occupancy charges.
- Admission and amusement charges.
- Receipts from sales of less than $0.11.
- Installment sales or other sales on credit made during the quarter.

NOTE: Businesses subject to Atlantic City luxury tax must include in gross receipts the "Total Gross Receipts" amounts reported on Line 1, Column B of Form ST-250 (Combined Atlantic City Luxury Tax/State Sales Tax Monthly Return) for each month of the quarter.

Do not include in gross receipts:

- Installment *payments* from installment sales or other sales on credit.
- Sales tax collected.
- Trade-in allowances.
- Sales of alcoholic beverages at wholesale.
- Receipts from lease transactions.

Adequate records should be maintained showing separately all exclusions from gross receipts.

Deductions
You may deduct the amount of all sales included in gross receipts which are not taxable under New Jersey law. No deduction may be taken for any amount which was not included in gross receipts on your return. Deductions may be taken only *once.* For example, if a deduction has been taken for an exempt clothing sale, you may not deduct the amount again as a sale of property which was delivered out of State.

Sales Jointly Taxable by Atlantic City and New Jersey. Businesses subject to Atlantic City luxury tax may deduct the "Taxable Receipts" amount from Line 3, Column B of the Combined Atlantic City Luxury Tax/State Sales Tax Monthly Return, Form ST-250.

Exempt Sales of Tangible Personal Property. Deduct the sales of any tangible personal property which is specifically exempt from sales tax (e.g., sales of grocery foods, clothing, etc.).

Exempt Sales of Services. Deduct total charges for services which are not subject to sales tax (e.g., professional services, personal services, etc.).

Exempt Occupancies. Deduct receipts from occupancies exceeding 90 consecutive days and occupancies for which the charge was $2 or less per day.

Exempt Admissions. Deduct any admission charges of $0.75 or less and admissions to sporting activities where a patron was a participant.

Sales Covered by Certificates. Deduct receipts from sales of property or services for which a valid New Jersey exemption certificate was accepted in lieu of tax.

INSTRUCTIONS FOR FILING THE NJ SALES TAX RETURNS

Returned Goods. Deduct the total sales price of taxable purchases returned by the customer. Include only the amounts refunded or credited to the customer. Do not include:

- Sales tax collected on returned purchases.
- Returns that were not subject to sales tax.
- Amounts not included in gross receipts on any return.

No deduction may be taken for returned goods which have been or will be deducted as an exempt sale on any sales and use tax return.

Property Delivered Out of New Jersey. Deduct total sales where the property was shipped to an out-of-State purchaser by common carrier, delivered to an out-of-State purchaser by the vendor in his own carrier, or delivered by the vendor to an out-of-State purchaser through an unregulated carrier hired by the vendor. Do not include sales of goods to an out-of-State purchaser if the customer took possession of the items in New Jersey.

Services Performed Outside of New Jersey. Deduct receipts from services performed outside of New Jersey.

Capital Improvements. Contractors may deduct sales of services which result in capital improvements to real property. Contractors are required to obtain a properly completed Certificate of Capital Improvement (Form ST-8) from customers for such transactions.

Rounding Off to Whole Dollars
Eliminate any amount under 50 cents and increase any amount 50 cents or over to the next higher dollar. Round amounts for the quarterly gross receipts and deductions lines only. No other lines are to be rounded.

Step-by-Step Instructions for Worksheet
Identification
New Jersey Taxpayer Identification Number. Enter your 12-digit New Jersey Taxpayer Identification Number as it appears on your New Jersey Certificate of Authority. If your ID number begins with the letters "NJ," enter "6," "5," and the remaining 10 digits. (Note: If you do not enter your ID number correctly, you will not be able to file.)

PIN/Taxpayer Name. Enter your 4-digit sales tax PIN (Personal Identification Number) or the first four characters of your registered taxpayer name. If you are entering your taxpayer name, use only letters and numbers. Omit symbols and spaces. (Note: If you do not enter your PIN or the first four characters of your taxpayer name correctly, you will not be able to file.)

Contact Phone Number. Enter the area code and phone number of a contact person for the taxpayer.

Tax Preparer's Identification Number. If the return is being filed by a tax preparer, enter the preparer's 9-digit Federal identification number or social security number. This information will be requested during the signature portion of the phone call.

Return Information
FORM ST-51 — MONTHLY RETURN
Complete this section if you are filing a monthly return for the first or second month of the quarter. *You are required to file a monthly return only if your tax liability for the month is more*

than $500. If you are filing a quarterly return, go to "Form ST-50 — Quarterly Return," below.

There are two monthly return sections on the worksheet; one for the first month of the quarter and one for the second month of the quarter. Complete the section that corresponds to the month for which you are filing.

Line 1 – Period Covered by Return. The two-digit number of the month (e.g., "01" for January, "02" for February) covered by the return is preprinted on this line of your worksheet. Enter the four-digit year in which the month fell in the boxes to the right of the month.

Line 2 – Amount of Tax Due. Multiply the total monthly taxable receipts (gross receipts minus deductions) by the sales tax rate. Do not include in gross receipts amounts collected for sales tax. Enter on Line 2 the larger of this figure or the actual amount of sales tax collected for that month. Also include any use tax that is due. Note: A monthly return cannot be filed by phone if the amount due is less than one dollar. Monthly payments of less than one dollar must be included with your quarterly return.

Line 3 – Penalty and Interest. Compute any penalty and interest charges incurred for late payment and/or late filing for the month and enter the amount on Line 3. If you are unable to determine this amount, enter "0." The State will calculate the penalties and interest and send you a bill.

Line 4 – Total Amount Due. The system will calculate the total amount due and provide the amount to you. Enter the amount stated on Line 4. Continue completing the worksheet with the "Payment Information" section. See instructions on page 4.

FORM ST-50 — QUARTERLY RETURN
Complete this section if you are filing for the third month of the quarter. A quarterly return must be filed even if no tax is due and/or no sales were made during the quarter.

Line 1 – Period Covered by Return. The number that reflects the calendar quarter covered by the return (e.g., "1" for the first quarter, "2" for the second quarter, etc.) is preprinted on this line of your worksheet. Enter the four-digit year in which the quarter fell in the boxes to the right of the quarter.

Line 2 – Gross Receipts for Quarter. Enter on Line 2 the total gross receipts (to the nearest dollar) from all transactions, including exempt transactions, which occurred during the three-month reporting period covered by the return. See "Gross Receipts" on page 2 for more information. If you had no gross receipts for the quarter, enter "0."

Line 3 – Deductions. Enter on Line 3 the amount of all sales (to the nearest dollar) included on Line 2 which are not taxable under New Jersey law. See "Deductions" on page 2 for more information. If you had no deductions for the quarter, enter "0."

Line 4 – Amount of Tax Collected. Enter on Line 4 the amount of sales tax collected for the quarter. If you did not collect any sales tax for the quarter, enter "0."

Line 5 – Sales Tax Due. The system will calculate the sales tax due and provide the amount to you. (The amount of sales tax due may be greater than the amount collected.) Enter the amount stated on Line 5.

SALES TAX RETURN
Instructions (Cont.)

Line 6 – Use Tax Due. Enter on Line 6 the total amount of use tax due for taxable tangible personal property or taxable services used during the quarter on which no sales tax was paid. (For more information request publication ANJ-7, *Use Tax in New Jersey*.) Also include here the total amount of use tax due on lease transactions. If you had no use tax liability for the quarter, enter "0."

NOTE: Direct payment permit holders enter the total sales and use tax liability on taxable purchases and uses during the quarter covered by the return.

Line 7 – Total Tax Due. The system will calculate the total tax due and provide the amount to you. Enter the amount stated on Line 7.

Line 8 – Total Monthly Payments. If you have already paid part of your quarterly liability with a monthly return (Form ST-51) for the first and/or second month of the quarter, or by electronic funds transfer, enter the total of these payments on Line 8. If you did not make any monthly payments for the quarter, enter "0."

Line 9 – Quarterly Amount Due. The system will calculate the sales and use tax balance due for the quarter and provide the amount to you. Enter the amount stated on Line 9. If your total monthly payments (Line 8) exceed the total tax due (Line 7), you may be eligible for a refund. (To obtain a refund you must file a Claim for Refund, Form A-3730, which is available online and by phone. See "Where to Get Information," below.) Enter "0" here and on Line 11 and continue filing the quarterly return.

Line 10 – Penalty and Interest. Compute any penalty and interest charges incurred for late payment and/or late filing for the quarter and enter the amount on Line 10. If you are unable to determine this amount, enter "0." You will be billed for any penalty or interest due.

Line 11 – Total Amount Due. The system will calculate the total amount due for the quarter and provide the amount to you. Enter the amount stated on Line 11. If you have a balance due, you can pay by e-check, credit card, or EFT. See "How to Pay" on page 1. You are not required to submit your payment on the same date as your telephone call, however, your payment must be made by the due date to avoid penalty and interest charges.

Payment Information

If you wish to pay by e-check, enter on the worksheet the 9-digit bank routing number, the account number (omit hyphens, spaces, symbols, and letters), the type of account, and the date you want the payment to be debited from your account. The earliest payment debit date you may select is the next business day. However, payment transactions initiated by 11:59 p.m. on the due date will be deemed timely even if the settlement date (date payment is debited from the account) is the next business day.

You can also pay by credit card or EFT after you have completed your telephone filing and received a Confirmation Number. See "How to Pay" on page 1.

Signature and Confirmation

Signature. You are required to affirm and sign your return by agreeing to the following statement and then providing a voice signature: "I verify and affirm that all tax information provided during this telephone call is correct. I am aware that if any of the information provided by me is knowingly false, I am subject to punishment." Your return cannot be processed without this affirmation or a signature. Tax preparers filing on behalf of clients will also be required to enter their tax identification number.

Confirmation Number. After you sign your return, stay on the line until the system assigns you a 7-digit Confirmation Number. This number serves as proof that your return was successfully filed. Enter the number and the date you filed your return in the boxes on the worksheet for the appropriate period along with the name of the person who "signed" the return. **Your return is not filed until you receive a Confirmation Number.**

If you make your quarterly payment by e-check in a separate telephone call, you will receive a separate Confirmation Number for the payment transaction.

Your Confirmation Number is your only proof that your return was successfully filed. Enter it on your worksheet and keep the worksheet for your business files for four years in case of audit. **Do not mail it to the Division of Taxation.**

Amended Returns

Errors on monthly returns (Forms ST-51) are to be adjusted on the quarterly return (Form ST-50) for that quarter. Errors on quarterly returns must be corrected by filing an amended return. You may amend a quarterly return through the Business Paperless Telefiling System or by completing a paper Amended Quarterly Sales Tax Return (Form ST-607A). If the correction results in an overpayment of tax for the quarter, file a Claim for Refund (Form A-3730). To obtain Form ST-607A or A-3730, visit the Division of Taxation Web site or call the Forms Request System. See "Where to Get Information," below.

Where to Get Information

By Phone
Call the Division of Taxation's Customer Service Center at **609-292-6400**. Representatives are available from 8:30 a.m. to 4:30 p.m., Monday through Friday (except holidays).

Online
- Division of Taxation Web site:
  www.state.nj.us/treasury/taxation/
- E-mail: **taxation@tax.state.nj.us**

Order Forms and Publications
To obtain copies of the EZ TeleFile Worksheet and Instructions, as well as other tax forms and publications:
- Call the Forms Request System from a Touch-tone phone at **1-800-323-4400** (within NJ, NY, PA, DE, and MD) or **609-826-4400** (anywhere).
- Call NJ TaxFax at **609-826-4500** from your fax machine's phone.
- Visit the Division of Taxation's Web site:
  www.state.nj.us/treasury/taxation/

In Person
Visit a New Jersey Division of Taxation Regional Office. For the address of the office nearest you, call the Automated Tax Information System from a Touch-tone phone at **1-800-323-4400** (within NJ, NY, PA, DE, and MD) or **609-826-4400** (anywhere) or visit our Web site.

SALES TAX RETURN
Instructions (Cont.)

In the sample form shown on page 45 you would be required to show why you did not collect tax on the $6,071. The State will more than likely audit (when they do) two or three years. This means that eight to twelve quarterly reports will be questioned for accuracy. You must be prepared to show the auditor substantiation for non-taxable sales. Some of the reasons for non-taxable sales might be one or more of the following:

1. **Proof on non-taxable sales (food, clothing, etc.)**

2. **Sales made out of State**

3. **Sales to a tax-exempt organization**

4. **Wholesale sales to retailers**

The State of New is very aggressive in their efforts to collect what is due them. If you cannot provide evidence as to why you did not collect tax, you will be required to pay it. Some of the forms needed to prove non-taxable sales are shown on the following pages.

If you have any questions concerning whether your products or services are taxable or what certificates should be utilized, simply contact the sales tax office nearest you. (See locations listed on page 43.)

At this point, we will review how your records should be kept to provide sufficient information regarding taxable and non-taxable sales.

It is necessary to maintain a record of your receipts or sales by differentiating between taxable and non-taxable sales.

Let's refer back to the Sales Tax form for the months of October, November and December. Here we reported a total sales figure of $18,500 and non-taxable of $6,071. In an audit, the agent reviews your sales tax forms and he/she will ask you to explain why you did not collect sales tax on the $6,071. If you have kept clear records, you simply only have to refer back to the sales or receipts journal to determine where the non-taxable sales were. For each non-taxable sale you need to have an exemption certificate on file or be able to prove an out-of-state sale.

As you can see from the sales journal on this page, the non-taxable sales total $6,071. You would need to keep on file one or more of the following forms: ST-3, ST-4, ST-7, ST-8, or ST-13. These certificates are filled out by the business owner who buys from you and does not pay sales tax. If you can produce these completed certificates, they will usually suffice for the auditor as proof of non-taxable sales.

DATE	INVOICE	TO	AMT	NON TAXABLE	TAXABLE	SALES TAX
10/3	1007	M-M CO	2000	2000		
10/15	1008	CERO-SMIT	1500		1500	105
10/22	1009	M-M CO	500	500		
11/3	1010	ROBYN INC	3100		3100	217
11/17	1011	AMELA CO	700	700		
12/1	1012	JSN CO	800	800		
12/19	1013	METRIC	900		900	63
12/26	1014	LN INC	9000	2071	6929	485
		TOTALS	18500	6071	12429	870

Some of these certificates can be explained as follows:

ST-3   **Resale Certificate — given to a wholesaler by the retailer. The retailer does not pay sales tax because he will resell the item to the final consumer. The final consumer pays the tax.**

ST-4   **Issued by the purchaser who is buying items that are tax exempt.**

ST-7   **Used by farmers for tax-exempt purchases.**

ST-8   **Issued by a homeowner to a contractor. The completed form exempts the homeowner from paying sales tax on capital improvements to the property.**

ST-13   **Issued by a contractor for exempt purchases of material used for real property.**

The forms substantiating non-taxable sales need only be completed once for each purchaser. As an example, one of your customers, the North Edison Little League, purchases hardware supplies from you several times a month. You must keep on file an ST-4 form signed by the Little League. Once you have the form, all subsequent sales are non-taxable by the same organization.

Some of the forms used to prove non-taxable sales are shown on the following pages.

ST-3 (11-99, R-10)

State of New Jersey
DIVISION OF TAXATION

SALES TAX
FORM ST-3

RESALE CERTIFICATE

PURCHASER'S NEW JERSEY
CERTIFICATE OF AUTHORITY NUMBER

To be completed by purchaser and given to and retained by seller. See instructions on back.
Seller should read and comply with the instructions given on both sides of an exemption certificate.

TO _____ Date _____
(Name of Seller)

_____
Address   City   State   Zip

The undersigned certifies that:

(1) He holds a valid Certificate of Authority (number shown above) to collect State of New Jersey Sales and Use Tax.

(2) He is principally engaged in the sale of (indicate nature of merchandise or service sold):

_____

(3) The merchandise or services being herein purchased are described as follows:

(4) The **merchandise** described in (3) above is being purchased: *(check one or more of the blocks which apply)*

    (a) ☐ For resale in its present form.

    (b) ☐ For resale as converted into or as a component part of a product produced by the undersigned.

    (c) ☐ For use in the performance of a taxable service on personal property, where the property which is the subject of this Certificate becomes part of the property being serviced or is later transferred to the purchaser of the service in conjunction with the performance of the service.

(5) The services described in (3) above are being purchased: *(check the block which applies)*

    (a) ☐ By a vendor who will either collect the tax or will resell the services.

    (b) ☐ To be performed on personal property held for sale.

I, the undersigned purchaser, have read and complied with the instructions and rules promulgated pursuant to the New Jersey Sales and Use Tax Act with respect to the use of the Resale Certificate, and it is my belief that the seller named herein is not required to collect the sales or use tax on the transaction or transactions covered by this Certificate. The undersigned purchaser hereby swears (under the penalties for perjury and false swearing) that all of the information shown in this Certificate is true.

_____
NAME OF PURCHASER   (as registered with the New Jersey Division of Taxation)

_____
(Address of Purchaser)

By _____
(Signature of owner, partner, officer of corporation, etc.)   (Title)

MAY BE REPRODUCED
(Front & Back Required)

FORM ST-3 RESALE CERTIFICATE

ST-4 (2-00, R-12)

State of New Jersey
DIVISION OF TAXATION

ELIGIBLE NONREGISTERED
PURCHASER: SEE INSTRUCTIONS **

SALES TAX

PURCHASER'S NEW JERSEY
CERTIFICATE OF AUTHORITY NUMBER

FORM ST-4

EXEMPT USE CERTIFICATE

To be completed by purchaser and given to and retained by seller.
Please read and comply with the instructions given on both sides of this certificate.

TO _____ Date _____
(Name of Seller)

_____
Address   City   State   Zip

The undersigned certifies that there is no requirement to pay the New Jersey Sales and/or Use Tax on the purchase or purchases covered by this Certificate because the tangible personal property or services purchased will be used for an exempt purpose under the Sales & Use Tax Act.

The tangible personal property or services will be used for the following exempt purpose:

The exemption on the sale of the tangible personal property or services to be used for the above described exempt purpose is provided in subsection N.J.S.A. 54:32B- [   ] (See reverse side for listing for principal exempt uses of tangible personal property or services and fill in the block with proper subsection citation).

I, the undersigned purchaser, have read and complied with the instructions and rules promulgated pursuant to the New Jersey Sales and Use Tax Act with respect to the use of the Exempt Use Certificate, and it is my belief that the seller named herein is not required to collect the sales or use tax on the transaction or transactions covered by this Certificate. The undersigned purchaser hereby swears under the penalties for perjury and false swearing that all of the information shown in this Certificate is true.

_____
NAME OF PURCHASER   (as registered with the New Jersey Division of Taxation)

_____
(Address of Purchaser)

By _____
(Signature of owner, partner, officer of corporation, etc.)   (Title)

MAY BE REPRODUCED
(Front & Back Required)

FORM ST-4 EXEMPT USE CERTIFICATE

ST-13 (11-99, R-5)

State of New Jersey
DIVISION OF TAXATION

SALES TAX

FORM ST-13

To be completed by owner of real property and contractor, and retained by contractor.

CONTRACTOR'S NEW JERSEY
CERTIFICATE OF AUTHORITY NUMBER

CONTRACTOR'S EXEMPT PURCHASE CERTIFICATE

_____
(Name of Seller)

_____
(Address of Seller)

The materials, supplies, or services purchased by the undersigned are for exclusive use in erecting structures, or building on, or otherwise improving, altering or repairing real property of the exempt organization, governmental entity, or qualified housing sponsor named below and are exempt from Sales and Use Tax under N.J.S.A. 54:32B-8.22.

THIS CONTRACT COVERS WORK TO BE PERFORMED FOR: (Check one)

☐ EXEMPT ORGANIZATION

Name of Exempt Organization . . . . _____

Address . . . . _____

Exempt Organization Number . . . . _____

☐ NEW JERSEY OR FEDERAL GOVERNMENTAL ENTITY

Name of Governmental Entity . . . . _____

Address of Governmental Entity . . . . _____

☐ QUALIFIED HOUSING SPONSOR

Name of Qualified Housing Sponsor . . . . _____

Address of Qualified Housing Sponsor . . _____

ADDRESS OR LOCATION OF CONTRACT WORK SITE:

_____

I, the undersigned contractor hereby verifies and affirms that all of the information shown on this certificate is true.

_____
Name of Contractor as registered with the New Jersey Division of Taxation

_____
Address of Contractor

_____
Signature of Contractor or Authorized Employee

See INSTRUCTIONS on reverse side.

MAY BE REPRODUCED
(Front & Back Required)

FORM ST-13 CONTRACTOR'S EXEMPT
PURCHASE CERTIFICATE

54

State of New Jersey
DIVISION OF TAXATION

SALES TAX
FORM ST-8

CERTIFICATE OF EXEMPT
CAPITAL IMPROVEMENT

To be completed by both owner of real property and contractor, and retained by contractor. Read instructions on back of this certificate. Do not send this form to the Division of Taxation.

A registered New Jersey contractor must collect the tax on the amount charged for labor and services under the contract unless the owner gives him a properly completed Certificate of Exempt Capital Improvement.

MAY BE ISSUED ONLY BY THE OWNER OF THE REAL PROPERTY
MAY NOT BE ISSUED FOR THE PURCHASE OF MATERIALS

_____
(Name of Contractor)

_____
(Address of Contractor)

_____
(Contractor's New Jersey Certificate of Authority Number)

THE FOLLOWING INFORMATION MUST BE FURNISHED:

The nature of the contract is as follows (describe the exempt capital improvement to be made):_____

_____

_____

_____

_____

The address or location where work is to be performed: _____

_____

TOTAL AMOUNT OF CONTRACT $ _____

The undersigned hereby certifies that he is not required to pay sales and use tax with respect to charges for installation of tangible personal property, because the performance of the contract will result in an exempt capital improvement to real property. The undersigned purchaser hereby affirms (under the penalties for perjury and false swearing) that all of the information shown in this Certificate is true.

CONTRACTOR'S CERTIFICATION	**PROPERTY OWNER'S SIGNATURE**
I certify that all sales and use tax due has been or will be paid by the undersigned on purchases of materials incorporated or consumed in the performance of the contract described herein.	_____ (Name of owner of real property) _____ (Address of owner of real property) By _____
_____ (Signature of Contractor) (Date)	_____ (Signature of owner, partner, (Date) officer of corporation, etc.)

Any person making representations on this certificate which are willfully false may be subject to such penalties as may be provided for by law.

REPRODUCTION OF CERTIFICATE OF EXEMPT CAPITAL IMPROVEMENT FORMS: Private reproduction of both sides of the Exempt Capital Improvement Certificates may be made without the prior permission of the Division of Taxation.

FORM ST-8 CERTIFICATE OF CAPITAL IMPROVEMENT

ST-7 (7-06, R-10)

State of New Jersey
DIVISION OF TAXATION

SALES TAX

Purchaser's New Jersey Tax Registration Number	Eligible Nonregistered Purchaser (See Instructions)

FORM ST-7

FARMER'S EXEMPTION CERTIFICATE

To be completed by purchaser and given to and retained by seller.

The seller must collect the tax on a sale of taxable property or services unless
the purchaser gives him a properly completed New Jersey exemption certificate.

TO _____ Date _____
(Name of Seller)

_____
(Address)

_____
(City)   (State)   (Zip)

Check applicable box:

☐ Single Purchase Certificate
☐ Blanket Certificate

The purchaser certifies that it is exempt from payment of the Sales and Use Tax on purchases to be made
from the seller because the property or service is to be used for an exempt purpose described in N.J.S.A.
54:32B-8.16 of the Sales and Use Tax Act as follows:

"Sales of tangible personal property and production and conservation services to a farmer for use and
consumption directly and primarily in the production, handling and preservation for sale of agricultural or
horticultural commodities at the farming enterprise of that farmer."

Description of agricultural or horticultural commodities produced at the purchaser's farmer enterprise:

_____

_____

Description of tangible personal property or service purchased: _____

_____

_____

_____
(Name of individual, partnership, association, or corporation)

_____
(Business address)

By _____
(Signature of individual farm owner, partner, officer of corporation or other qualified representative)

INSTRUCTIONS

This certificate must be presented to a seller when making an exempt purchase. The farmer's exemption does
not apply to purchases which will not be used directly and primarily in farm production. The purchases of
automobiles, certain other motor vehicles, natural gas, electricity and any materials used to build a building or
structure (except silos, greenhouses, grain bins and manure handling facilities) are taxable regardless of the
intended use on a farm or by a farmer.

MAY BE REPRODUCED
(Front & Back Required)

FORM ST-7 FARMER'S EXEMPTION CERTIFICATE

8
PAYROLL REPORTING TO THE INTERNAL REVENUE SERVICE AND THE STATE OF NEW JERSEY

In this section on payroll reporting, I will explain some of the payroll reports that must be filed with the I.R.S. and the State of New Jersey. It is important that you be aware of what taxes you are liable for, when they are due, and at what point in time you must inform the federal and state agencies that you have employees.

Payroll Reporting to the Internal Revenue Service

As soon as you have your first employee (full- or part-time), you will need to determine how much tax should be withheld from his/her gross pay. The I.R.S. supplies employers with a booklet called *Circular E*, and it can be obtained from any I.R.S. office. This small pamphlet shows you how much federal withholding tax and social security should be withheld from each employee's pay check. The I.R.S. has requirements for sending them the Federal Withholding Tax and Social Security withheld from your employees.

At least every three months (at the end of a three-month quarter) you are required to prepare and submit a 941 form. On this form you show how much tax was withheld from the employee's gross pay and remit the amount to the I.R.S. If the taxes withheld from employees exceed $500 in any month, you must pay these taxes monthly by using a Federal Tax Deposit Card. This form is shown on the next page. When you file the 941 form, you can take credit for any monthly payment made. Once again, these forms are tough to learn on your own, so let an accountant show you how to complete them the first time.

For any Federal Business Tax information contact the local I.R.S. office at (631) 447-4955 or Fax at (631) 447-8960.

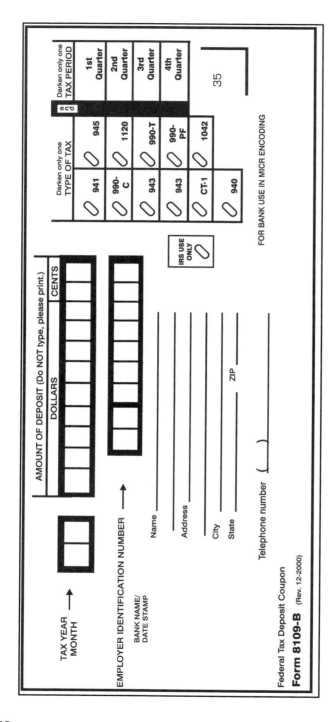

FEDERAL TAX DEPOSIT FORM
PAYROLL TAXES

58

Form 941 for 2006: Employer's QUARTERLY Federal Tax Return

(Rev. January 2006)

Department of the Treasury — Internal Revenue Service

990106

OMB No. 1545-0029

(EIN)
Employer identification number ☐☐ – ☐☐☐☐☐☐☐

Name (not your trade name)

Trade name (if any)

Address
Number   Street   Suite or room number
City   State   ZIP code

Report for this Quarter ...
(Check one.)

☐ 1: January, February, March

☐ 2: April, May, June

☐ 3: July, August, September

☐ 4: October, November, December

Read the separate instructions before you fill out this form. Please type or print within the boxes.

Part 1: Answer these questions for this quarter.

1 Number of employees who received wages, tips, or other compensation for the pay period including: *Mar. 12* (Quarter 1), *June 12* (Quarter 2), *Sept. 12* (Quarter 3), *Dec. 12* (Quarter 4) **1**

2 Wages, tips, and other compensation **2**

3 Total income tax withheld from wages, tips, and other compensation **3**

4 If no wages, tips, and other compensation are subject to social security or Medicare tax . ☐ Check and go to line 6.

5 Taxable social security and Medicare wages and tips:

	Column 1		Column 2
5a Taxable social security wages		× .124 =	
5b Taxable social security tips		× .124 =	
5c Taxable Medicare wages & tips		× .029 =	

5d Total social security and Medicare taxes (*Column 2*, lines 5a + 5b + 5c = line 5d) . **5d**

6 Total taxes before adjustments (lines 3 + 5d = line 6) **6**

7 TAX ADJUSTMENTS (Read the instructions for line 7 before completing lines 7a through 7h.):

7a Current quarter's fractions of cents . . . .

7b Current quarter's sick pay . . . .

7c Current quarter's adjustments for tips and group-term life insurance

7d Current year's income tax withholding (attach Form 941c) . . .

7e Prior quarters' social security and Medicare taxes (attach Form 941c)

7f Special additions to federal income tax (attach Form 941c) . . .

7g Special additions to social security and Medicare (attach Form 941c)

7h TOTAL ADJUSTMENTS (Combine all amounts: lines 7a through 7g.) **7h**

8 Total taxes after adjustments (Combine lines 6 and 7h.) **8**

9 Advance earned income credit (EIC) payments made to employees **9**

10 Total taxes after adjustment for advance EIC (line 8 – line 9 = line 10) **10**

11 Total deposits for this quarter, including overpayment applied from a prior quarter . . . **11**

12 Balance due (If line 10 is more than line 11, write the difference here.) **12**
Make checks payable to *United States Treasury*.

13 Overpayment (If line 11 is more than line 10, write the difference here.) ☐ Check one ☐ Apply to next return.
☐ Send a refund.

▶ You **MUST** fill out both pages of this form and **SIGN** it.

Next ➡

For Privacy Act and Paperwork Reduction Act Notice, see the back of the Payment Voucher.   Cat. No. 17001Z   Form **941** (Rev. 1-2006)

I.R.S. FORM 941 — EMPLOYERS QUARTERLY FEDERAL TAX RETURN

Payroll Reporting to the State of New Jersey

Like any other state agency, New Jersey has a form to be completed for payroll-reporting procedures. In New Jersey you are required to notify the state as soon as your gross payroll reaches $1,000. This will also alert the Division of Unemployment and Disability so that your employee will be eligible for benefits. If you did not complete a NJ-REG form when you started your business, you do that and answer question one with the appropriate informaiton. If you had already completed a form NJ-REG, you file an amended application and answer the questions on page two.

From your employees you are obligated to withhold the New Jersey Gross Income Tax and a combination of Unemployment/Disability. You may contact the New Jersey Department of Labor and Industry, CN 390, Trenton, New Jersey 08625 to obtain the N.J.G.I.T. withholding tax tables. At the time this book was written, New Jersey also required the employee to pay .0925% of his/her gross pay toward unemployment/disability to the state for wages paid up to $26,600. The employer withholds this from the employee's gross pay, and matches it according to a formula based on claims made by former employees for unemployment and/or disability benefits.

New Jersey requires a quarterly reporting just as the I.R.S. and there are two forms that must be completed and mailed at the end of a three-month quarter. They are the NJ-927 and NJ500. The NJ-500 reports monthly withholding tax and the NJ-927 reports quarterly wages, withholding tax, and is used to remit payments for unemploymnet and disability amounts.

If your New Jersey Gross income tax withheld from employees exceeds $500 per month, you must file monthly. On the next page is a copy of the form so that you may become familiar with it.

Remember, as soon as you have employees, it will be necessary to begin filing the necessary forms with the I.R.S. and the State of New Jersey. Don't delay doing this, as you are subject to penalties for non-filing and interest for all withholding taxes not paid timely.

Just a reminder. In all states you are obligated to carry worker's compensation insurance as soon as you hire your first employee.

You may obtain information regarding worker's compensation by calling (609) 292-2516 or writing to the

Division of Worker's Compensation
Department of Labor
CN381
Trenton, New Jersey 08625

STATE OF NEW JERSEY - DIVISION OF TAXATION		NJ-500	Monthly Remittance of Gross Income Tax Withheld
WITHHOLDING PERIOD	DUE DATE		
August 2007	September 15 , 2007		

JAMY'S DONUT SHOPPE
44 DONNA COURT
CLARK, NJ 07066

|.|.|.||..||..|..||..||.|.|.|.|.|.|.||..||
GROSS INCOME TAX
PO BOX 248
TRENTON NJ 08646-0248

REMITTANCE AMOUNT

$ [.   ]

0112022345938000000HAND010810

N.J. GROSS INCOME TAX FORM

State Of New Jersey
Employer's Quarterly Report
NJ-927

		1. Total of All Wages Paid Subject to UI, DI, WF & HC	

Quarter Ending: Report Due:
09-30-2007   10-30-2007

2. Wages in Excess of First $26,600.00
3. Taxable Wages UI, WF & HC. Line 1 Minus Line 2
4. Taxable Wages Subject to DI   S

JAMY'S DONUT SHOPPE
44 DONNA COURT
CLARK, NJ 07066

5. Total UI, WF & HC Contributions Multiply Line 3 by Total UI, WF, & HC Rate   0.018250
6. Total DI Contributions Multiply Line 4 by DI Rate   0.007500
7. Total GIT Withheld (From Line 4 on Back)

Make Check Payable to:
Display return address in envelope window.

|..||...||.||...||..||...||.|||..||..||.|.|.||..||.|
State of New Jersey NJ-927
PO Box 632
Trenton, NJ 08646-0632

8. Total Liability (Add Lines 5, 6, & 7)
9. Total Payments & Credits
10. Overpayment Amount   Credit | Refund
11. Balance Due

927002235778520001BILL040908

N.J. PAYROLL TAX FORM FOR PAYING
UNEMPLOYMENT & DISABILITY

STATE OF NEW JERSEY
DIVISION OF REVENUE
BUSINESS REGISTRATION APPLICATION
Please read instructions carefully before filling out this form
ALL SECTIONS MUST BE FULLY COMPLETED

* NO FEE REQUIRED *

MAIL TO:
CLIENT REGISTRATION
PO BOX 252
TRENTON, NJ 08646-0252

OVERNIGHT DELIVERY:
CLIENT REGISTRATION
847 ROEBLING AVENUE
TRENTON, NJ 08611

FAX:
(609) 292-4291

A. Please indicate the reason for your filing this application (Check only one box)
- ☐ Original application for a new business
- ☐ Application for a new location of an existing registered business
- ☒ Amended application for an existing business
- ☐ Moved previously registered business to new location (REG-C-L can be used in lieu of NJ-REG)
- ☐ Applying for a Business Registration Certificate

Name and NJ Registration Number of your existing business: _____

B. FEIN # ☐☐ ☐☐☐☐☐☐☐ OR Soc. Sec. # of Owner | 1 | 2 | 3 | 4 | 5 | 6 | 7 | 8 | 9 |
☐ Check Box if "Applied for"

C. Name JON and AMY CARLIN
(If INCORPORATED - give Corp. Name; IF NOT - give Last Name, First Name, MI of Owner, Partners)

D. Trade Name JAMY'S DONUT SHOPPE

E. Business Location: (Do not use P.O. Box for Location Address)

Street 44 DONNA COURT

City CLARK   State | N | J |

Zip Code | 0 | 7 | 0 | 6 | 6 | 1 | 2 | 3 | 4 |
(Give 9-digit Zip)
(See instructions for providing alternate addresses)

F. Mailing Name and Address: (if different from business address)

Name _____

Street _____

City _____ State ☐☐

Zip Code ☐☐☐☐☐ ☐☐☐☐
(Give 9-digit Zip)

G. Beginning date for this business: __1__ / __1__ / __07__ (see instructions)   O/C ____
                                      month   day   year

H. Type of ownership (check one):
- ☐ NJ Corporation ☐ Sole Proprietor ☒ Partnership ☐ Out-of-State Corporation ☐ LLP ☐ Other ____
- ☐ Limited Partnership ☐ LLC (1065 Filer) ☐ LLC (1120 Filer) ☐ LLC (Single Member) ☐ S Corporation (You must complete page 41)

I. New Jersey Business Code | 5 | 3 | 0 | 6 | (see instructions)

FOR OFFICIAL USE ONLY

J. County / Municipality Code | 2 | 0 | 0 | 2 | (see instructions) K. County UNION
(New Jersey only)

DLN _____

L. Will this business be open all year? ☒ Yes ☐ No

CORP # _____

If NO - Circle months business will be open:
JAN FEB MAR   APR MAY JUN   JUL AUG SEPT   OCT NOV DEC
 ☐   ☐   ☐   ☐   ☐

M. IF A CORPORATION, complete the following:

Date of Incorporation: ____ / ____ / ____   State of Incorporation ☐☐ Fiscal month ☐☐
                       month day   year

Is this a Subsidiary of another corporation? ☐ YES ☐ NO   NJ Business/Corp. # ☐☐☐☐ ☐☐☐☐ ☐

If YES, give name and Federal ID# of parent: _____

N. Standard Industrial Code ☐☐☐☐ (If known)   O. NAICS ☐☐☐☐☐☐ (If known)

P. Provide the following information for the owner, partners or responsible corporate officers. (If more space is needed, attach rider.)

NAME (Last Name, First, MI)	SOCIAL SECURITY NUMBER / TITLE	HOME ADDRESS (Street, City, State, Zip)	PERCENT OF OWNERSHIP
CARLIN, JON	111-11-1111	26 EAST WAY, LINCROFT	50
	PARTNER	NEW JERSEY 07738	
CARLIN, AMY	222-22-2222	26 EAST WAY, LINCROFT	50
	PARTNER	NEW JERSEY 07738	

BE SURE TO COMPLETE NEXT PAGE

- 17 -

N.J. REG - AMENDED RETURN
TO REPORT NEW PAYROLL

FEIN#: _____ **NAME:** JAMY'S DONUT SHOPPE _____ **NJ-REG**

Each Question Must Be Answered Completely

1. a. Have you or will you be paying wages, salaries or commissions to employees working in New Jersey within the next 6 months? .... ☒ Yes ☐ No

    Give date of first wage or salary payment: $\frac{2}{\text{Month}}$ / $\frac{1}{\text{Day}}$ / $\frac{07}{\text{Year}}$

    If you answered "No" to question 1.a., please be aware that if you begin paying wages you are required to notify the Client Registration Bureau at PO Box 252, Trenton NJ 08646-0252, or phone (609)-292-1730.

   b. Give date of hiring first NJ employee: $\frac{2}{\text{Month}}$ / $\frac{1}{\text{Day}}$ / $\frac{07}{\text{Year}}$

   c. Date cumulative gross payroll exceeds $1,000 $\frac{2}{\text{Month}}$ / $\frac{8}{\text{Day}}$ / $\frac{07}{\text{Year}}$

   d. Will you be paying wages, salaries or commissions to New Jersey residents working outside New Jersey?........................... ☐ Yes ☒ No

   e. Will you be the payer of pension or annuity income to New Jersey residents?.. ☐ Yes ☒ No

   f. Will you be holding legalized games of chance in New Jersey (as defined in Chapter 47 Rules of Legalized Games of Chance) where proceeds from any one prize exceed $1,000?.. ☐ Yes ☒ No

   g. Is this business a PEO (Employee Leasing Company)? (If yes, see page 6).. ☐ Yes ☒ No

2. Did you acquire ☐ Substantially all the assets; ☐ Trade or business; ☐ Employees; of any previous employing units?............... ☐ Yes ☒ No
    If answer is "No", go to question 4.
    If answer is "Yes", indicate by a check whether ☐ in whole or ☐ in part, and list business name, address and registration number of predecessor or acquired unit and the date business was acquired by you. (If more than one, list separately. Continue on separate sheet if necessary.)

			PERCENTAGE ACQUIRED
Name of Acquired Unit _____	N.J. Employer ID	☐ Assets	_____ %
_____		☐ Trade or Business	_____ %
Address _____	Date Acquired	☐ Employees	_____ %

3. Subject to certain regulations, the law provides for the transfer of the predecessor's employment experience to a successor where the whole of a business is acquired from a subject predecessor employer. The transfer of the employment experience is required by law.

    Are the predecessor and successor units owned or controlled by the same interests?.. ☐ Yes ☒ No

4. Is your employment agricultural?... ☐ Yes ☒ No

5. Is your employment household?.. ☐ Yes ☒ No

   a. If yes, please indicate the date in the calendar quarter in which gross cash wages totaled $1,000 or more_____ / _____ / _____
   (Month   Day   Year)

6. Are you a 501(c)(3) organization?.. ☐ Yes ☒ No

7. Were you subject to the Federal Unemployment Tax Act (FUTA) in the current or preceding calendar year?...................... ☐ Yes ☒ No

    (See instruction sheet for explanation of FUTA) If "Yes", indicate year: _____

8. a. Does this employing unit claim exemption from liability for contributions under the Unemployment Compensation Law of New Jersey? ..... ☐ Yes ☒ No

    If "Yes," please state reason. (Use additional sheets if necessary) _____

   b. If exemption from the mandatory provisions of the Unemployment Compensation Law of New Jersey is claimed, does this employing unit wish to voluntarily elect to become subject to its provisions for a period of not less than two complete calendar years?.............. ☐ Yes ☒ No

9. Type of business   ☐ 1. Manufacturer   ☐ 2. Service   ☐ 3. Wholesale
                        ☐ 4. Construction   ☒ 5. Retail   ☐ 6. Government

    Principal product or service in New Jersey only BAKED GOODS _____

    Type of Activity in New Jersey only BAKERY _____

10. List below each place of business and each class of industry in New Jersey, even though you may have only one place of business or engage in only one class of industry.

    a. Do you have more than one employing facility in New Jersey?... ☐ Yes ☒ No

NJ WORK LOCATIONS (Physical location, not mailing address)		NATURE OF BUSINESS (See Instructions)			No. of Workers at Each Location and/in Each Class of Industry
Street Address, City, Zip Code	County	NAICS Code	Principal Product or Service Complete Description	%	
44 DONNA COURT, CLARK, NJ 07066	UNION	5306	BAKED GOODS	100	THREE

(Continue on separate sheet, if necessary)
BE SURE TO COMPLETE NEXT PAGE

N.J. REG - AMENDED RETURN TO REPORT NEW PAYROLL
(CONTINUED)

STATE OF NEW JERSEY NEW HIRE REPORTING FORM

Please mail to: New Jersey New Hire Operations Center, PO Box 4654, Trenton, NJ 08650-4654

TO ENSURE ACCURACY, PLEASE PRINT (OR TYPE) NEATLY IN UPPER-CASE LETTERS AND NUMBERS, USING A DARK, BALL POINT PEN

EMPLOYER FEDERAL EIN   —

EMPLOYER INFORMATION:

Employer Name _
(name, d/b/a, etc.)

Employer Payroll Address

_ _

_ _

Employer Payroll City   State   Zip Code + 4 (optional)

_   _ _   _ _ _ _   _ _ _ _

EMPLOYEE INFORMATION:

Employee Social Security Number   _ _ _ - _ _ - _ _ _ _

First   Last
Name _ _ _ _ _ _ _ _ _ _ MI (opt.) _   Name _ _ _ _ _ _ _ _ _ _ _ _ _ _ _ _ _ _

Employee Address

_ _

_ _

City   State   Zip Code + 4 (optional)

_   _ _   _ _ _ _   _ _ _ _

Date of Hire (optional)   Date of Birth (if available)   Gender (optional)

_ _   _ _   _ _ _ _   _ _   _ _   _ _ _ _   ☐ Male   ☐ Female
M M   D D   Y Y Y Y   M M   D D   Y Y Y Y

THIS FORM MAY BE REPRODUCED

N.J. NEW HIRE FORM

64

Forms, Fees, & Instructions

Division of Revenue   NJBGS

Instructions for Completing Employer Payroll Tax Form NJ-927

General Instructions

The NJ-927 Form has been revised for reporting periods starting with the report for the 3rd quarter of 1998 (report due October 30, 1998). The revised form will be scanned and imaged using automated character recognition technologies to input the information you supply. Please read and follow all instructions carefully.

The New Jersey Taxpayers' Bill Of Rights

The Taxpayers' Bill of Rights became law as P.L. 1992,c.175. The intent of the legislation is to insure that all taxpayers receive the information and assistance they need to understand and meet their State tax responsibilities and to insure that they receive fair and equal treatment in their dealings with the New Jersey Division of Taxation. By extension, the Division of Revenue is committed to complying with this legislation.

Information on the Taxpayers' Bill of Rights is available through the Division of Taxation. Call 1-800-323-4400 (Touch-tone phones within New Jersey only) or (609) 588-2525 (Touch-tone phones anywhere) to order Taxation's publication, ANJ-1, New Jersey Taxpayers' Bill of Rights (ANJ-1).

Customer service representatives are available at both the Division of Taxation and the Department of Labor to answer specific tax questions about the Gross Income Tax (Taxation) and Unemployment and Disability Insurance (Division of Employer Accounts). Those general information phone numbers are:

Division of Employer Accounts Hotline (609) 633-6400
Division of Taxation Hotline (609) 292-6400

You can find information, and answers to frequently asked questions on the following Web sites:

NJ Division of Taxation - http://www.state.nj.us/treasury/taxation
NJ Department of Labor - http://www.state.nj.us/labor

INSTRUCTIONS FOR COMPLETING
THE N.J. TAX FORM 927

N.J. Department of Labor
Division of Employer Accounts
PO Box 256
Trenton, N.J 08625-0256

STATE OF NEW JERSEY
EMPLOYER REPORT OF WAGES PAID
Read instructions on reverse side of employer's copy before completing this report.

WR-30 (R-7-04)

New Jersey Employer Registration Number:			Quarter Ending		Report Due		Tape Auth. No.	

Federal Employer I.D. Number:

Municipal Code: Industry Code:

Total No. of Employees Reported		Total Gross Wages Reported	$	

	(1) Employee Social Security Number	(2) Employee Name (Last, First, MI)	(3) Gross Wages Paid	(4) Base Weeks During Which Employee Earned $ ____ or more
1				
2				
3				
4				
5				
6				
7				
8				
9				
10				
11				
12				
13				
14				
15				
16				

I certify the information in thi report is true and correct.

X _____
(Signature)

_____
(Title)

_____
(Date)

(_____) _____
[Telephone]

Do Not Use This Form To Make Additions or Corrections
MAY BE REPRODUCED

Page _____ of _____ Pages

THE N.J. STATUS REPORT OF WAGES PAID

INSTRUCTIONS FOR FILING THE EMPLOYER REPORT OF WAGES PAID (WR-30)

1. GENERAL INSTRUCTIONS

The Division of Revenue will issue pre-printed wage reporting forms (Form WR-30) to all New Jersey employers who reported 100 or fewer employees in the previous quarter. Since pre-printed forms contain the name and Social Security Number of each employee, employers need to record only gross wages paid and base weeks earned within the data boxes on the form. The employee information on the pre-printed Form WR-30 should not be substituted by attaching a separate printout. For new employees, each pre-printed WR-30 will have an ADD Form on the back of the page. The ADD Form must be used to add new employees who are being reported for the first time. Employees must be added, even if you reported them under the federal New Hire Program. The New Hire Program became effective March 5, 1998 and is federally mandated. If you have questions about the New Hire Program, please call (toll free) 877-NJ- HIRES. Please do not use the front of the form to add employees.

Total Gross Wages Reported This Quarter: Enter the total gross wages paid to all employees included in the report for this quarter.

Total New Employees ADDED: Enter the total number of new employees you included on the ADD Form.

Total Employees Reported This Quarter: Add the number of new employees to the number of employees pre-printed on the WR-30. Enter the total number of employees (minus those deleted) to be reported for this quarter.

A. Social Security Number

The Social Security Number for each of your employees should be pre-printed in Column A on the form, if it was reported for the previous quarter. The Social Security Number should read exactly as it appears on the employee's Social Security Card. If the employee's Social Security Number is incorrect, fill in the oval in Column C, and enter all the employee's correct information on the ADD page.

B. Employee Name

The employee name should be pre-printed in the following sequence: Last Name, First Name, Middle Initial in Column B of the employee portion of the report. The employee name and Social Security Number should appear only once on any quarterly return. To correct an employee's name, fill in the oval in Column C, and enter all the employee's correct information on the ADD page.

C. Delete Column

On the re-designed Form WR-30, the delete column is now Column C (an oval shaped box) located between the Employee Name and Quarterly Gross Wages Paid columns. If an employee listed should not be reported, fill in the oval in Column C.

D. Quarterly Gross Wages Paid

Enter the employee gross wages within the data boxes in Column D, "Quarterly Gross Wages Paid." Please do not use commas, decimal points or any other symbols in or between the boxes. If no wages were paid, enter zero (0). Leaving this column blank will generate a penalty.

E. Base Weeks

Enter in Column E the number of base weeks during which the employee earned remuneration in an amount equal to or more than the amount shown above Column E on the front of the form. Base weeks listed for an employee can not exceed the maximum allowable base weeks shown in the message box on Form WR-30. If an employee did not earn any base weeks for the quarter being reported, you must enter a zero (0). Leaving this column blank will generate a penalty.

9
INCORPORATING YOUR BUSINESS IN NEW JERSEY

I like to tell a story of the business owner who comes to me to set up the books for a new corporation. My first question is always: Why did you incorporate? The answer varies and goes something like this — "Well, I thought it was a good idea" or "My friends told me I needed a corporation" or "I read somewhere that it would save me taxes."

There are many reasons to incorporate and just as many not to do it. Before you make the decision to incorporate, make sure you know why you are making the decision.

When you incorporate, you get permission from the State to create a separate business entity that can operate a business in N.J. This new entity has the right to enter into contracts, sue or be sued, and own property. Ownership of the corporation is shown by shares of stock issued to the stockholders.

The major advantages are as follows:

1. **You can limit your liability**
   If you incorporate, under most situations, your personal assets are safe from obligations incurred by the corporation. But the corporate form will not limit your liability for wrongdoings or on loans which you may have personally guaranteed.

2. **Lower tax rates**
   Depending on your personal income, the corporation may be advantageous to keep your taxes to a minimum.

3. **Raise capital through sale of stocks and bonds**
   The corporate structure allows the owners to raise money by selling stocks and borrow money through bond sales.

4. **Sometimes easier to borrow money**
   As a corporation, the lending institutions may charge a higher

rate of interest than that allowed to an individual. The bank, therefore, may be willing to lend your corporation money because they can collect more interest.

5. **Welfare plans**
In many situations, the corporation will be able to deduct expenditures that would not be allowed as a sole proprietor or partnership. Examples are: medical bills, disability insurance, and group life insurance when included in qualified welfare programs for employees.

6. **Easy to transfer ownership**
You can sell ownership in the corporation by transferring your shares of stock.

7. **Continued existence**
Once formed, the corporation continues regardless of who may own the stock. But in reality, the corporation may actually be worthless if the major controlling stockholder is unable to work in the business.

8. **High pension plan deductions**
Presently, the corporate structure may allow greater pension plan expenses than a sole proprietor or partnership.

9. **Looks classy to your customers**
The corporate structure and name shown with Inc. or Corp. following the title infers a large company. This type of title may impress people more than a sole proprietor.

The disadvantages are:

1. **Initial costs are high**
The expenses to incorporate a business are significantly higher than starting a sole proprietor or partnership. Costs range from $100 to $1,000 depending on your business and the amount of work completed by your attorney.

2. **Professional fees are costly**
The accounting and legal fees to maintain a corporation are much more expensive than those of a sole proprietor or partnership.

3. **High taxes**
   In many instances, you will have to pay corporate taxes to the I.R.S. and the State of New Jersey.

4. **Higher payroll taxes**
   The stockholders receiving compensation from the corporation will be considered employees and must pay Federal Social Security and New Jersey Unemployment. The corporate structure will result in higher payroll taxes than the sole proprietor or partnership organization.

5. **May be personally liable**
   Even though the business is incorporated and has limited liability, you may still be required to sign personally for loans and contracts.

If you decide to incorporate or form an LLC in the State of New Jersey, you need to file and complete the Public Records Filing form. The form can be obtained from the State web site at https://www.nj.gov/treasury/revenue/gettingregistered.htm. You may also use the site to complete the applicaiton and form your new business entity on line.

You may also fax a completed form to the State Treasurer at 609-984-6851. Be sure to include a cover letter with your requested business name, a return fax number, and your personal credit card information.

Obtaining a Name for Your Corporation or Limited Liability Company

By calling the New Jersey State Treasurer, Division of Commercial Recording, you can do a search of potential names for your Corporation or Limited Partnership within minutes. The Division has recently installed a new telephone system with several options. The phone number is 1-609-292-9292.

You may also check the availability of a name by visiting the NJ web site at: http://www.state.nj.us/treasury/revenue/checkbusiness.htm.

STATE OF NEW JERSEY
DIVISION OF REVENUE

"FEE REQUIRED"   **PUBLIC RECORDS FILING FOR NEW BUSINESS ENTITY**

Fill out all information below INCLUDING INFORMATION FOR ITEM 11, and sign in the space provided. Please note that once filed, this form constitutes your original certificate of incorporation/formation/registration/authority, and the information contained in the filed form is considered <u>public</u>. Refer to the instructions for delivery/return options, filing fees and field-by-field requirements. Remember to remit the appropriate fee amount. Use attachments if more space is required for any field, or if you wish to add articles for the public record.

1. **Business Name:**   JON and AMY CARLIN

2. **Type of Business Entity:** ___ ___ ___
   (See Instructions for Codes, Page 21, Item 2)

3. **Business Purpose :**
   (See Instructions, Page 22, Item 3)

4. **Stock** (<u>Domestic</u> Corporations only; LLCs and Non-Profit leave blank):

5. **Duration** (If Indefinite or Perpetual, leave bank):

6. **State of Formation/Incorporation** (Foreign Entities Only):

7. **Date of Formation/Incorporation** (Foreign Entities Only):

8. **Contact Information:**
   Registered Agent Name:

   <u>Registered Office:</u>
   (Must be a New Jersey <u>street</u> address)

   Street _____

   City _____ Zip _____

   Main Business or Principal Business Address:

   Street _____

   City _____ State_____ Zip _____

9. **Management** (Domestic Corporations and Limited Partnerships Only)
   - For-Profit and Professional Corporations list initial Board of Directors, minimum of 1;
   - Domestic Non-Profits list Board of Trustees, minimum of 3;
   - Limited Partnerships list all General Partners.

Name	Street Address	City	State	Zip

The signatures below certify that the business entity has complied with all applicable filing requirements pursuant to the laws of the State of New Jersey.

10. **Incorporators** (Domestic Corporations Only, minimum of 1)

Name	Street Address	City	State	Zip

Signature(s) for the Public Record (See instructions for Information on Signature Requirements)

Signature	Name	Title	Date

CERTIFICATE OF INCORPORATION

INSTRUCTIONS FOR BUSINESS ENTITY PUBLIC RECORD FILING

GENERAL INSTRUCTIONS AND DELIVERY/RETURN OPTIONS

1. Type or machine print all Public Records Filing forms, and submit with the correct FEE amount. (See FEE schedule on page 22).

2. Choose a delivery/return option:

   a. **Regular mail** - If you are sending work in via regular mail, use the correct address:

   > New Jersey Department of the Treasury
   > Division of Revenue/Corporate Filing Unit
   > PO Box 308
   > Trenton, NJ 08625-0308

   All processed mail-in work will be returned via regular mail. Providing a self-addressed return envelope will speed processing. Otherwise, on a cover letter, indicate the return address if other than the registered office of the business entity.

   b. **Expedited/Over-the-Counter** - If you are expediting a filing (8.5 business hour processing), make sure that you deliver over-the-counter to: 225 W. State Street, 3rd Floor, Trenton, NJ 08608-1001, or have a courier/express mail service deliver to this address. Do not use USPS overnight delivery. Be sure to provide instructions as to how the filing is to be sent back to you: regular mail; front desk pick-up at 225 W. State Street; or delivery by courier/express mail. If you use a courier or express mail service for return delivery, be sure to provide a return package and completed air bill showing your name or company name (in the "to" and "from" blocks) and your courier account number.

   Notes: Use an acceptable payment method for mail and over-the-counter work:

   - Check or money order payable to the Treasurer, State of NJ;
   - Credit card -MASTERCARD/VISA or DISCOVER (provide card number, expiration date and name/address of card holder);
   - Depository account as assigned by the Treasurer; or
   - Cash.

   For over-the-counter **AND** mail-in submissions, remember to provide the required number of copies of the Public Record Filing. Filings for for-profit entities are submitted in duplicate and non-profit filings are done in triplicate.

   c. **Facsimile Filing Service (FFS)** - Transmit your filings to (609) 984-6851. You may request 8.5 business hour processing (EXPEDITED SERVICE), or same business day processing (SAME DAY SERVICE). Processing includes document review, fee accounting and acknowledgment turnaround.

   Payment Methods - You may pay for services via credit card (Master Card/Visa, Discover and American Express) or depository account (one payment method per request).

   Delivery/Turnaround - *Barring difficulties beyond the Division of Revenue's control, including those that affect the Division of Revenue's data communication or data processing systems,* all EXPEDITED requests delivered to the FFS workstation between 8:30 a.m. and 5:00 p.m. on workdays will be processed and returned within 8.5 business hours, while SAME DAY requests delivered by 12:00 noon on work days will be processed by 5:00 p.m. the same day. Requests received during off hours, weekends or holidays will be processed on the next work day, in 8.5 business hours. In the event of down time, upon system recovery, requests will be processed in receipt date/time order.

   Cover Sheet - with your transmission, send a cover sheet entitled
   > New Jersey Department of the Treasury
   > Division of Revenue
   > Facsimile Filing Service Request

   The cover sheet must include work request details: Name of firm or individual transmitting the service request; date of submission; depository account number or credit card number with expiration date; description of service requested e.g., "Certificate of Incorporation"; business name associated with the filing (proposed name for a new business entity); desired service level (EXPEDITED or SAME DAY); total number of pages in the request transmission, including cover sheet; and fax back number.

Note: The Division of Revenue will accept one filing per FFS. Requests lacking cover sheets or required cover sheet information may be rejected. Requests that do not contain a fax back number will not be processed. Also, if a service level is not specified, the Division of Revenue will assume that the request is for EXPEDITED service.

The Division of Revenue will make three attempts to transmit to the fax back number you provide. If the transmissions are unsuccessful, the Division of Revenue will send acknowledgments of completed filings to the registered office of the business entity involved via regular mail; or hold rejections in a pending file for two weeks, and dispose of the material thereafter.

Receiving Processed Work Back - For accepted work, the Division of Revenue will enter your Public Records Filing and Consolidated Registration application, and fax back an FFS Customer Transmittal with a copy of the approved Public Records Filing form stamped "FILED". For rejected work, the Division of Revenue will fax a FFS Customer Transmittal and Rejection Notice. If your submission is rejected, correct all defects and resubmit your filing as a new FFS request.

PAGE 23 INSTRUCTIONS

LINE BY LINE REQUIREMENTS FOR Public Records FILING

Item 1   **Business Name** - Enter a name followed by an acceptable designator indicating the type of business entity--for example: Inc., Corp., Corporation, Ltd., Co., or Company for a corporation; Limited Liability Company or L.L.C. for a Limited Liability Company; Limited Partnership or L.P. for a Limited Partnership; Limited Liability Partnership or L.L.P. for a Limited Liability Partnership.

Note: The Division of Revenue will add an appropriate designator if none is provided.

Remember that the name must be distinguishable from other names on the State's data base. The Division of Revenue will check the proposed name for availability as part of the filing review process. If desired, you can reserve/register a name prior to submitting your filing by obtaining a reservation/registration. For information on name availability and reservation/registration services and fees, visit the Division's Web site at http://www.state.nj.us/njbgs/ or call (609) 292-9292 Monday - Friday, 8:30 a.m.- 4:30 p.m.

Item 2   **Type of Business Entity** - Enter the two or three letter code that corresponds with the type of business you are forming/registering:

Statutory Authority	Entity Type	Type Code
Title 14A	Domestic Profit	DP
For-Profit Corp.	Domestic Professional	PA
	Foreign Profit	FR
	(Incl. Foreign Professional Corp.)	
	Foreign Profit	DBA
	"Doing Business As"	
Title 15A	Domestic Non-Profit	NP
Non-Profit Corp.	Foreign Non-Profit	NF
Title 42:2B	Domestic LLC	LLC
Limited Liability Co.	Foreign LLC	FLC
Title 42:2A	Domestic LP	LP
Limited Partnership	Foreign LP	LF
Title 42		
Limited Liability	Domestic LLP	LLP
Partnership	Foreign LLP	FLP

N.J. INCORPORATING INSTRUCTIONS

Item 3 **Business Purpose** - Provide a brief description of the business purpose for the public record. If the business is a domestic for-profit corporation, you may leave this field blank and thereby rely on the general purpose clause provided in N.J.S.A. 14A: "The purpose for which this corporation is organized is(are) to engage in any activity within the purposes for which corporations may be organized under N.J.S.A. 14A:1-1 et seq."

Item 4 **Stock** - Domestic for-profit corporations only, list total shares.

Item 5 **Duration** - List the duration of the entity. If the duration is indefinite or perpetual, leave the field blank.

Item 6 **State of Formation/Incorporation**- Foreign entities only, list home state.

Item 7 **Date of Formation/Incorporation** - Foreign entities only, list the date of incorporation/formation in home state.

Item 8 **Contact Information** - Provide the following information:
a) **Registered Agent** - Enter one agent only. The agent may be an individual or a corporation duly registered, and in good standing with the State Treasurer.

b) **Registered Office** -Provide a New Jersey street address. A PO Box may be used only if the street address is listed as well.

c) **Main Business Address** - List the main or principal business street address in New Jersey.

Item 9 **Management** - For profit and professional corporations list initial Board of Directors, minimum of 1; domestic non-profits list Board of Trustees, minimum of 3; limited partnerships list all General Partners.

Item 10 **Incorporators** - Domestic profit, professional and non-profit corporations only, list incorporators, minimum of 1.

Signature Requirements for Public Records Filing:
The incorporator(s) and only the incorporator(s) may sign domestic profit, professional and non-profit corporate filings. Only the president, VP or Chief Executive Officer may sign foreign corporate filings. ALL general partners must sign limited partnership filings. ANY authorized representative may sign domestic or foreign limited liability company filings, while any authorized partner may sign domestic or foreign limited liability partnership filings.

PAGE 24 INSTRUCTIONS

Item 11 Provide additional "Entity-Specific" information as applicable.

Nonprofit corporations wanting Federal IRC section 501(c)(3) status are advised to consult the IRS concerning IRS required wording. The IRS telephone number is 1-877-829-5500, and the website is at www.irs.gov.

CHECKLIST FOR PUBLIC RECORDS FILING
- Completed and signed Public Records Filing (pages 23 and 24) (*Note: Use appropriate envelope supplied - P.O. Box 308*)
- Completed and signed Business Registration Application (pages 17-19) (*NOTE: Use appropriate envelope supplied-PO Box 252*).
- Filing fee using an acceptable payment method.
- Transmittal letter or service request sheet with instruction for returning completed work (mail and over-the-counter requests)
- Completed and signed CBT-2553 (S Corporation Election) if applicable
- Cover sheet listing work request details (FAX Filing Requests)

CHECKLIST FOR BUSINESS REGISTRATION APPLICATIONS
- Completed and signed Registration Application (pages 17-19)
- Completed and signed NJ-REG-L (Cigarette and Motor Fuel Wholesalers/Distributors/Manufacturers only) or CM-100 (Cigarette and Motor Fuel Retailers only, if applicable).

Delivery Options for:

Public Records Filings:		**Business Registration Application:**	
Mail:	PO Box 308, Trenton, NJ 08625	Mail:	PO Box 252, Trenton, NJ 08646-0252
Over-The-Counter:	225 W. State Street, 3rd Floor		Overnight: 847 Roebling Avenue, Trenton, NJ 08611
	Trenton, NJ 08608-1001	FAX:	(609) 292-4291
Phone:	(609) 292-9292		
FAX:	(609) 984-6851		

FEE SCHEDULE
(Revised 7/1/02)

FAX FILING FEES (FFS)
- Each EXPEDITED FFS request is subject to a $15 fee, plus 1.00 per page fee for all accepted filings that are FAXED back for all Title 14A, Title 15A, and LP transactions.
  For LLCs and LLPs, each EXPEDITED FFS request is subject to a $25 fee, plus 1.00 per page fee for all accepted filings that are FAXED back.
- Each SAME DAY FFS request is subject to a $50 fee, plus a 1.00 per page fee, for all accepted filings that are FAXED back.
- These fees are in addition to the basic statutory fees associated with the filing itself.

BASIC FILING FEES
- Filing fee for all domestic entities, except non-profits, is $125 per filing; non-profit filing fee is $75 per filing.
- Filing fee for all foreign entities is $125 per filing.

SERVICE FEES AND OTHER OPTIONAL FEES (All added to basic filing fee, if selected.)
- Expediting Service Fee (8.5 business hours) is $15 per filing request for Title 14A, Title 15A and LP transactions.
- Expediting Service Fee (8.5 business hours) is $25 per filing request for LLCs and LLPs.
- Same Day Fee is $50 per filing request.
- Alternate Name Fee is $50 for each name.
- FAX Page Transmission Fee is 1.00 per page for all filings that are FAXED back.
- Certified Copies of Accepted Filings are $25 for each filed entity.

NOTE: THERE IS NO FILING FEE REQUIRED TO FILE FORM NJ-REG

N.J. INCORPORATING INSTRUCTIONS
(CONTINUED)

10
ASSISTANCE AVAILABLE TO HELP YOU GET STARTED

In recent years federal, state and local governments have begun to realize the importance of helping the small business owner. These various agencies have instituted and sponsored many programs to help the entrepreneur obtain money and learn about taxes. Almost all of the new assistance programs are without cost to the small business person. This section will concern itself with the government-sponsored groups, what they can do for you, and their locations in the State.

Your taxes are used to keep these groups active, so don't be afraid to seek out their help. All of the individuals involved in these programs have business experience and are interested in helping you make your business a success.

FEDERAL GOVERNMENT
SMALL BUSINESS ADMINISTRATION — S.B.A.

Every state has at least one S.B.A. district office staffed by a group of experts in financial, management and procurement assistance. These individuals are responsible for delivering S.B.A. programs to the state's small business community.

Some of these programs include direct and guaranteed loans to different groups. Borrowers in these programs may be small business concerns which cannot borrow from conventional lenders, minority or socially disadvantaged small business owners, and disaster victims.

The New Jersey District office is responsible for the delivery of SBA's many programs and services to 21 counties in NJ. Office hours are Monday - Friday 8:00 a.m. until 4:30 p.m.

74

SERVICES AVAILABLE:

1. Financial assistance through guaranteed loans made by area banks and lenders

2. Assistance to businesses owned by socially and economically disadvantaged individuals through 3(a) programs.

3. Free consulting through the network of Small Business Development Services

4. Free counseling, advice, and information through SCORE - Counselors To America's Small Business

5. Women's Business Centers (WBCs) provide a wide range of servces to women entrepreneurs.

6. Business Information Centers (BICs) provide tools for new business or for existing businesses that need assistance in expanding or improving.

7. Special loan programs are available for businesses involved in international trade.

The S.B.A. office for the State of New Jersey is located at:

Two Gateway Center, 5th Floor, Newark, New Jersey 07102
(973) 645-2434

INTERNAL REVENUE SERVICE ASSISTANCE

The I.R.S. also prints a number of publications dealing with various federal taxes. These materials can be obtained from local I.R.S. offices or on-line at www.irs.gov. Some of the guides that may be of interest to the small business person are:

NUMBER	TITLE
334	Tax Guide for Small Business
505	Tax Withholding and Estimated Tax
535	Business Expenses and Operating Loss
539	Withholding Taxes and Reporting Requirements
541	Tax Information on Partnerships
542	Tax Information on Corporations
552	Record Keeping Requirements
560	Tax Information on Self Employed
583	Record Keeping for a Small Business
587	Business Use of Your Home
589	Information on Sub Chapter S Corporations

Taxpayer assistance is available from the I.R.S. by calling the local office. The I.R.S. also holds several tax workshops during the year at offices around the State. You may contact any one of the following I.R.S. offices for more information.

Internal Revenue Service Locations in New Jersey
The Taxpayer Advocate Service: Call (973)921-4043 in Springfield
or 1-877-777-4778 elsewhere.

Atlantic County
5218 Atlantic Ave.
Mays Landing, NJ 08330
(609) 625-0678,

Bergen County
1 Kalisa Way
Paramus, NJ 07652
(201) 634-7052

Camden County
57 Haddonfield Road
Cherry Hill, NJ 08002
(856) 321-1328

Essex County
970 Broad Street
Newark, NJ 07102
(973) 645-6690

Hudson County
30 Montgovery Street
Jersey City, NJ 07302
(201) 332-9110

Mercer County
44 So. Clinton Ave. 3rd Floor
Trenton, NJ 08608
(609) 989-0533

Middlesex County
100 Dey Place, Wick Plaza
Edison, NJ 08817
(732) 572-9752

Monmouth County
4 Paragon Way.
Freehold, NJ 07728
(732) 660-0063

Morris County
Mt. Pleasant Office Bldg.
1719 Route 10 East
Parsippany, NJ 07054
(973) 808-0921

Passaic County
200 Federal Plaza
Paterson, NJ 07505
(973) 357-4114

Union County
200 Sheffield Street
Mountainside, NJ 07092
(908) 301-2112

W. Essex County
165 Passaic Avenue
Fairfield, NJ 07004
(973) 808-0821

SCORE - Counselors to America's Small Business

Individuals who are already in business or who are planning on going into business can obtain FREE counseling from SCORE. Sponsored by the Small Business Administration, SCORE is a network of volunteer business executives and professionals - mostly retired, but some still active - that provides small business with advice and counsel. There is no charge for SCORE counseling. For further information and/or assistance, contact the SCORE location nearest you or visit the NJ web site at: http://www.nj-score.org.

S.C.O.R.E. CHAPTERS
Web site for New Jersey SCORE Chapters: http://www.nj-score.org

New Jersey SCORE
Raritan Valley Comm College
Route 28 & Lamington Road
North Branch, NJ 08876
Phone: (908) 218-8874

Newark SCORE
Two Gateway Center, 15th Floor
Newark, NJ 07102
Phone: (973) 645-3982

Sussex County Community College
Alliance for Corporate & Commmunity
Education
One College Hill Bldg. D
Newton, NJ 07860
Phone: 973) 300-2140

Brookdale SCORE
Brookdale Comm College
765 Newman Springs Road
Lincroft, NJ 07738
Phone: (732) 224-2568

Eastern Monmouth Area Chamber of Commerce
170 Broad Street
Red Bank, NJ 07701
Phone: (732) 741-0055

Bergen County SCORE
Community Services Bldg.
327 E. Ridgewood Avenue
Paramus, NJ 07652
Phone: (201) 599-6090

Ocean County SCORE
Dover Twp. Municipal Bldg.
33 Washington Street
Toms River, NJ 08753
Phone: (732) 505-6033

Camden County SCORE
c/o Summit Bank
4900 Ste. 70
Pennsauken, NJ 08109-4792
Phone: (856-) 486-3421

Greater Princeton SCORE
216 Rockingham Row
Princeton Forrestal Village
Princeton, NJ 08540
Phone: (609) 520-1776

Conectiv
5100 Harding Highway
Mays Landing, NJ 08330
Phone: (609) 909-5339

Small Business Incubator
900 Briggs Road
Mt. Laurel, NJ 08054
Phone: (856) 486-3421

Business Information Center
Camden County College/Camden Campus
200 N. Broadway, 3rd Floor, Rm 319
Camden, NJ 08102
Phone: (856) 338-1817, x-3162

Camden County Store - Echelon Mall
Somerdale & Burnt Mills Road, 2nd Floor
Voorhees, NJ 08043
Phone: (856) 486-3421

Main Street Development
2214 Pacific Avenue /PO Box 1781
Wildwood, NJ 08260
Phone: (609) 729-6818

Air Services Development Office
Building 80, 2nd Floor
Newark, NJ 07102
Phone: (973) 961-4278

New Jeresy Economic Dev. Corp.
30 Montgovery Street
Jersey City, NJ 07302
Phone: (201) 333-7797

Montclair Economic Dev. Corp.
50 Church Street
Montclair, NJ 07042
Phone: (973) 783-8003

NJ Economic Development Authority
36 West State Street
Trenton, NJ 08625
Phone: (609) 520-1776

Unitied National Bank
675 Franklin Boulevard
Somerset, NJ 08875
Phone: (732) 745-5050

Summit Bank Building
2 Centre Drive
Jamesburg, NJ 08831
Phone: (609) 520-1776

Sayreville Municipal Building
167 Main Street
Sayreville, NJ 08872
Phone: (732) 390-2922

Monmouth County Library
125 Symnes Drive
Manalapan, NJ 07726
Phone: (732) 431-7220

Monmouth County Library
Eastern Branch - Hwy 35
Shrewsbury, NJ 07701
Phone: (732) 842-5995

Southern Monmouth Chamber of Commerce
Old Mill Plaza
2100 Highway 35, Suite E-23
Sea Girt, NJ 08750
Phone: (732) 974-1151

Wall Township Library
2700 Allaire Road
Wall, NJ 07719
Phone: (732) 449-8877

Western Monmouth Chamber of Commerce
17 Broad Street
Freehold, NJ 07719
Phone: (732) 462-3030

Northern Monmouth Chamber of Commerce
500 State Highway 36, Suite 204/205
Navesink, NJ 07752
Phone: (732) 291-7870

Fairleigh Dickinson University
285 Madison Avenue
Madison, NJ 07940
Phone: (973) 443-8801

Morris County Chamber of Commerce
25 Lindsley Drive, Suite 105
Morristown, NJ 07960
Phone: (973) 539-3882

County College of Morris
Route 10 & Center Grove Road
Student Center
Randolph, NJ 07869
Phone: (973) 328-5187

Picatinny Arsenal Innovation Center
3159 Schrader Road
Dover, NJ 07869
Phone: (973) 442-6400

Southern Ocean County Chamber of Commerce
265 West Ninth Street
Ship Bottom, NJ 08008
Phone: (609) 494-7211

Clifton Community Center
1232 Main Avenue
Clifton, NJ 07011
Phone: (973) 470-5956

Tri-County Chamber of Commerce
2055 Hamburg Turnpike
Wayne, NJ 07470
Phone: (973) 831-7788

Greater Paterson Chamber of Commerce
100 Hamilton Plaza
Patterson, NJ 07505
Phone: (973) 881-7300

Suburban Chambers of Commerce
71 Summit Avenue
Summit, NJ 07901
Phone: (908) 522-1700

Union Township Chamber of Commerce
355 Chestnut Street
Union, NJ 07083
Phone: (908) 688-2777

Greater Elizabeth Chamber of Commerce
Independence Community Bank
456 N. Broad Street
Elizabeth, NJ 07208
Phone: (908) 355-7600

STATE PROGRAMS
Small Business Assistance Office

The Office of Small Business Assistance was recently established with the New Jersey Department of Commerce and Economic Development. Some of the functions of this office are:

1. **Establishment of a loan referral program for small business**

2. **Keep in close contact with the Department of the Treasury to promote contracts with small business firms**

3. **Receive complaints from small businesses**

4. **Study laws affecting small businesses**

For assistance contact:

Office of Small Business Assistance
New Jersey Department of Commerce &
  Growth Commission
Mary Roebling Bldg.
20 W. State St., CN 835
Trenton, New Jersey 08625
(609) 984-4442

The office of Promoting Technical Innovation is located in the New Jersey Department of Commerce and Growth Commission. The office was established to stimulate and encourage the development of new commercial products to be manufactured in New Jersey. The services provided include: communication among inventors, sources of capital, technical consultations, information on available research and development grants, and assistance in the preparation of applications.

For assistance contact:

Office of Promoting Technical Innovation
New Jersey Department of Commerce & Growth Commission
Trenton, New Jersey 08625   (609) 292-7138

Small Business Development Centers

Small Business Development Centers (SBDC) are state-operated programs, funded jointly by the U.S. Small Business Administration (SBA) and the State government hosting the program. These centers serve as an umbrella under which resources are collected for the exclusive use of small business owners and future entrepreneurs.

The centers provide one-on-one counseling and training in management and financial planning through public and private sources, trade and business associations, and students and faculty associated with universities or colleges in which S.B.D.C.'s are generally located. The locations in New Jersey are:

NJSBDC HEADQUARTERS
Rtugers Business School
Ms. Brenda B. Hopper, State Director
49 Bleeker Street
Newark, NJ 07102
(973) 353-1927 • FAX: (973) 353-1110
e-mail: bhopper@njsbdc.com

ATLANTIC/CAPEMAY COUNTIES
Small Business Development Center
Comectiv Office Building
Mr. R. Joseph Molineaux, Director
5100 Harding Highway
Mays Landing, NJ 08330
(609) 909-5339 • FAX: (609) 909-9671

BERGEN COUNTY COMMUNITY COLLEGE
Small Business Development Center
Mr. Vincent D'Elia, Director
Ciarco Learning Center
355 Main St.
Hackensack, NJ 07601
(201) 489-8670

MONMOUTH/OCEAN
Mr. Bill Nunnally, Director
Brookdale Community College
Library 246
765 Newman Springs Road
Lincroft, NJ 07738
(732) 842-8685 • FAX: (732) 842-0203

KEAN UNIVERSITY
Small Business Development Center
Ms. Mira Kostak, Director
Willis Hall, 301 Morris Avenue
Union, NJ 07083
(908) 737-4220 • FAX: (980) 527-2960

MERCER/MIDDLESEX
Small Business Development Center
Ms. Lorraine Allen, Director
36 South Broad Street
Trenton, NJ 08608
(609) 989-5232 • FAX: (609) 989-7638

NEW JERSEY CITY UNIVERSITY
Small Business Development Center
Ms. Barbara S. O'Neal, Director
20 College Street
Jersey City, NJ 07301
(201) 200-2156 • FAX: (201) 200-3404

RARITAN VALLEY COMMUNITY COLLEGE
Small Business Development Center
Ms. Sue Johnson, Director
Route 28 and Lamington Road
North Branch, NJ 08876
(908) 526-1200 Ext. 8516 • FAX:(908) 725-9687

RUTGERS UNIVERSITY - NEWARK CAMPUS
Small Business Development Center
Mr. Tandai Ndoro, Regional Director
43 Bleeker Street
Newark, NJ 07102
(973) 353-5950 • FAX: (973) 353-1030

RUTGERS UNIVERSITY -CAMDEN CAMPUS
Small Business Development Center
Mr. Gary Rago, Director
Waterfront Technology Center
200 Federal Street
Camden, NJ 08102
(856) 225-6221 • FAX: (856) 225-6621

WARREN COUNTY - CENTENARY COLLEGE
Warren County Chamber of Commerce
Mr. Jim Smith, Director
400 Jefferson Street
Brotherton Hall - Room 25
Hackettstown, NJ 07840
(908) 852-1400 Ext. 2136

WILLIAM PATERSON UNIVERSITY
Small Business Development Center
Ms. Kate Muldoon, Director
131 Ellison Street
Paterson, NJ 07505
(973) 754-8695

NJSBDC SPECIALTY PROGRAMS

International Trade	**Procurement**	**Technology**
(800) 432-1565	(973) 353-1414	Randy Harmon
		(973) 353-1932

LOCAL & STATEWIDE ASSISTANCE

Many people who start their own business don't know whom to contact for information on local licenses, permits, and occupancy information. The most helpful group in your area would be the Chamber of Commerce. These groups are organized specifically to assist businesses wanting to start a venture in the chamber's area of location. The various Chambers of Commerce throughout the state are listed on the following pages.

Another organization recently formed is the S.B.A.Certified Development Corporation which is presently located in counties throughout the state. These groups assist in loan applications, sponsor seminars, and keep the business owners in the county informed of changes in the laws.

SBA CERTIFIED DEVELOPMENT CORPORATIONS

NEW JERSEY BUSINESS FINANCE CORPORATION
185 Bridge Plaza North, Suite 211
Fort Lee, New Jersey 07024
Ira Lutsky, President
 (201) 346-0300

CORPORATION FOR BUSINESS ASSISTANCE IN NJ
36 West State Street
Trenton, New Jersey 08625
Contact: William C. Moody
(609)777-4898

PARTICIPATING LENDERS & TECHNICAL ASSISTANCE PROVIDERS

Greater Newark Business Development Consortium
744 Broad Street, 26th Floor
Newark, NJ 07102
Executive Director: Mark Quinn
(973)242-4132

Trenton Business Assistance Corp.
247 E. Front Street
Trenton, NJ 08611
Executive Director: Deborah Osgood
(609)396-2595

Union County Economic Development Corp.
Liberty Hall Corporate Center
1085 Morris Ave., Suite 531
Union, NJ 07083
Executive Director: Maureen Tinen
(908)527-1166

CHAMBERS OF COMMERCE IN NEW JERSEY

State of New Jersey: New Jersey State Chamber of Commerce
216 West State Street, Trenton, N.J. 08608
(609) 989-7888, Fax: (609) 989-9696
Hispanic Chamber of Commerce: (201) 451-9512

Aberdeen: (see Matawan)
Asbury Park: P.O. Box 649, 07712, (732) 775-7676
Atlantic City: 1125 Atlantic Ave., 08401, (609) 345-5600
Avalon: 30th & Ocean Dr., 08202, (609) 967-3936
Bamber Lake: (see Forked River)
Bay Head: (see Point Pleasant)
Bayonne: 621 Ave. C, P.O. Box 266, 07002, (201) 436-4333
Belleville: PO Box 284, 07109, (973) 759-4848
Belmar: 1005^1/2 Main St., P.O. Box 297, 07719, (732) 681-2900
Bergenfield: 35 Washington Ave., 07621, (201) 387-8300
Berkeley Heights: (see Summit)
Bloomfield: 277 Broad St., 07003, (973) 748-2000
Bloomingdale: P.O. Box 100, 07403, (973) 838-1104
Boonton: P.O. Box 496, 07005, (973) 334-4117
Bogota: 60 W. Main, PO Box 215, 07603
Bordentown: 11 Walnut St., P.O. Box 65, 08505, (609) 298-7774
Bound Brook: P.O. Box 227, 08805, (732) 356-7273
Brick: 270 Chambers Bridge Rd., 08723, (732) 477-4949
Bridgeton: 53 S. Laurel St., P.O. Box 1063, 08302, (609) 455-1312
Brigantine: P.O. Box 484, 08203, (609) 266-3437
Budd Lake: 98 Route 46, Village Green Annex, P.O. Box 192, 07828, (973) 691-0109
Burlington: P.O. Box 67, 08016, (609) 387-0963
Burlington County: (see Mt. Laurel)
Butler: (see Bloomingdale)
Caldwell: (see W. Caldwell)
Cape May: 513 Washington St. Mall - 2nd Floor, P.O. Box 556, 08204, (609) 884-5508
Cape May Court House: PO Box 6, 08210, (609) 463-1655
Cedar Grove: (see West Caldwell)

Carney's Point: 91A S. Virginia Ave., 08069, (856) 299-6699
Chatham: P.O. Box 231, 07928, (973) 635-2444
Cherry Hill: 1060 N. Kings Hwy., 08034 (856) 667-1600
Clifton: P.O. Box 110, 07011, (973) 470-9300
Colts Neck: (see Freehold)
Cranford: 8 Springfield Ave., P.O. Box 165, 07016, (908) 272-6114
Dennis Township: (see Ocean View)
Denville: P.O. Box 333, 07834 (973) 627-1340
East Brunswick: P.O. Box 56, 08816, (732) 257-3009
Eastern Monmouth: 170 Broad St.,Red Bank 07701, (732) 741-0055
East Orange: P.O. Box 731, 07019, (973) 674-0900
Eatontown: (see Red Bank)
Edison: 100 Menlo Park #209, 08817, (732) 494-0300
Egg Harbor City: P.O. Box 129, 08215, (609) 965-0260
Elizabeth:135 Jefferson Ave., P.O. Box 300, 07207-0300, (908) 352-0900
Elmwood Park: 511 Boulevard, 07407, (201) 797-5008
Englewood: 2-10 N. Van Brunt St., 07631, (201) 567-2381
Englewood Cliffs: P.O. Box 954, 07632, (201) 567-9344
Fair Lawn: 0-100 27th St., 07410, (201) 796-7050
Fairview: 202 Anderson Ave., 07022, (201) 945-3707
Farmingdale: P.O. Box 534, 07727, (732) 919-0149
Forked River: 103 Route 9 N., P.O. Box 306, 08731, (609) 693-8312
Fort Lee: 210 Whitman St., 07024, (201) 944-7575
Franklin Lakes: P.O. Box 149, 07417, (201) 891-7609
Franklin Township: 1717 Amwell Rd., Somerset, 08873-2746,
        (732) 873-1717
Garfield: P.O. Box 525, 07026, (973) 773-7500
Glassboro: PO Box 651, 08028, (609) 881-7900
Glen Rock: P.O. Box 176, 07452, (201) 447-3434
Hackensack: 302 Union St., 07601, (201) 489-3700
Hackettstown: P.O. Box 546, 07840, (908) 852-1253
Hammonton: 10 S. Egg Harbor Rd., P.O. Box 554, 08037, (609) 561-9080
Hasbrouck Heights: PO Box 1, 07604, (201) 599-5822
Hawthorne: 471 Lafayette Ave., P.O. Box 331, 07507, (973) 427-5078
Hightstown: P.O. Box 87, 08520, (609) 448-4412
Hillside: PO Box 965, 07205, (908) 946-5130
Howell: P.O. Box 196, 07731, (732) 363-4114
Irvington: P.O. Box 323, 07111, (973) 372-4100
Jersey City: 253 Washington St., 07302, (201) 435-7400
Kearney: 764 Kearney Ave., 07032, (201) 991-5600
Keyport: PO Box 785, 07735, (732) 264-3626
Lake Hopatcong: P.O. Box 64, 07849 (973) 361-2810
Lakewood: 395 Hwy 70 #125, 08701, (732) 363-0012
Lambertville: 239 N. Union St., 08530, (609) 397-0055
Lanoka Harbor: (see Forked River)

Lebanon: 2200 Route 31, Suite 15, 08833, (908) 735-5955
Ledgewood: P.O. Box 436, 07852, (973) 770-0740
Livingston: 154 S. Livingston Ave., 07039, (973) 992-4343
Lodi: P.O. Box 604, 07644, (973) 777-9687
Long Branch: 628 Broadway, 07740, (732) 222-0400
Madison: P.O. Box 152, 07940, (973) 377-7830
Mahwah: P.O. Box 506, 07430
Manahawkin: (see Ship Bottom)
Manasquan: P.O. Box 365, 08736, (732) 223-8303
Maplewood, PO Box 423, 07040 (201) 761-4333
Marlboro: (see Freehold)
Matawan: P.O. Box 522, 07747, (732) 290-1125
Maywood: 140 W. Pleasant Ave., 07607, (201) 843-3111
Metuchen: 323 Main St., 08840, (732) 548-2964
Middletown: Union Square Mall, P.O. Box 424, 07748, (732) 671-3360
Midland Park: P.O. Box 267, 07432, (973) 423-5815
Millburn: P.O. Box 651, 07041, (973) 379-1198
Millville: 100 N. High St., P.O. Box 831, 08332 (856) 825-2600
Montclair: 26 Parks St., #2025, 07042, (973) 744-7660
Montville: 195 Change Bridge Rd., 07045, (973) 263-3310
Morristown: 25 Lindsley Dr., 07960, (973) 539-3882
Mount Freedom: PO Box 391, 07970, (973) 361-3462
New Brunswick: 1091 Aaron Rd., North Brunswick, 08902, (732) 821-1700
New Brunswick: 123 Church St., 08901, (732) 545-4800
New Providence: (see Summit)
Newark: 744 Broad St, 26th Floor, 07102, (973) 242-4209
Newton: 120 Hampton House Rd., 07860, (973) 579-1811,
North Caldwell: (see West Caldwell)
Northern Monmouth: 500 Hwy 36, Navesink 07752, (732) 291-7870
Nutley: 610 Franklin Ave., 07110, (973) 667-5300
Oakland: P.O. Box 8, 07436, (201) 337-7117
Ocean City: P.O. Box 157, 08226, (609) 399-1412
Ocean County: (see Toms River)
Ocean Grove: P.O. Box 415, 07756, (732) 774-1391
Oceanview: PO Box 85, 08230, (609) 624-2276
Old Bridge: P.O. Box 5241, 08857, (732) 607-6340
Orange: POBox 1178, 07050, (973) 676-8725
Paramus: P.O. Box 325, 07652, (201) 261-3344
Parsippany: 959 Rte. 46 #101, 07054, (201) 402-6400
Passaic: (see Clifton)
Paterson: 100 Hamilton Plaza, 07505, (973) 881-7300
Perth Amboy: 214 Smith St., 08862, (973) 442-7400
Phillipsburg: 675 Corliss Ave., 08865, (908) 859-5161
Piscataway: 1 Possumtown Rd., 08854, (732) 394-0220
Plainfield: 120 W. 7th St., 07060, (908) 754-7250

Point Pleasant: 517 A. Arnold Ave., 08742, (732) 899-2424
Pompton Lakes: PO Box 129, 07442, (973) 839-0187
Princeton: Princeton Forrestal Village, 216 Rockingham Row, 08540, (609) 520-1776
Rahway: P.O. Box 595-C, 07065, (732) 429-0555
Randolph: (see Mount Freedom)
Raritan: P.O. Box 236, 08869, (908) 429-0555
Ridgewood: 199 Dayton St., 07450, (201) 445-2600
Ringwood, 109 Skyline Dr., P.O. Box 62, 07456, (973) 835-7998
Roxbury: (see Ledgewood)
Rutherford: P.O. Box 216, 07070, (201) 933-5230
Saddlebrook: 50 Market St. 07663, (201) 556-0123
Salem: (see Carney's Point)
Sayreville: (see Old Bridge)
Short Hills: (see Millburn)
Somerset: 15 Cedar Grove Ln. #9-A, 08873, (973) 560-3737
Somerville: P.O. Box 833, 08876, (732) 725-1552
South Amboy: (see Old Bridge)
Southern Monmouth: P.O. Box 1305, Wall 07719, (732) 974-1151
Southern Ocean: 265 W. 9th St., Ship Bottom 08008, (609) 494-7211
South Orange: P.O. Box 621, 07079, (973) 762-4333
Sparta: P.O. Box 444, 07871, (973) 729-7700
Stone Harbor: PO Box 422, 08247, (609) 368-6101
Summit: P.O. Box 824, 07902, (908) 522-1700
Sussex County: (see Newton)
Tenafly: 78 County Rd., P.O. Box 163, 07670, (201) 894-0568
Toms River: 1200 Hooper Ave., 08753, (732) 349-0220
Towaco: (see Clifton)
Trenton: 214 W. State St., 08608, (609) 393-4143
Union: 355 Chestnut St., 07083, (908) 688-2777
Vernon: PO Box 308, 07462, (973) 764-0764
Vineland: P.O. Box 489, 08360-0489, (856) 691-7400
Voorhees: Piazza 6014 at Main St., 08043, (856) 424-7776
Wayne: 2055 Hamburg Turnpike, 07470, (973) 831-7788
West Caldwell: 3 Fairfield Ave., 07006, (973) 226-5500
Western Monmouth: 17 Broad St., Freehold 07728, (732) 462-3030
West Hudson: (see Kearny)
West Milford: P.O. Box 234, 07480, (973) 728-3150
West New York: 428 60th St., P.O. Box 1145, 07093, (201) 295-5065
Westfield: P.O. Box 81, 07090, (908) 233-3021
Westwood: P.O. Box 155, 07675, (201) 664-8468
Wildwood: 3601 Boardwalk, 08260, (609) 729-4000
Woodbridge: 52 Main St., 07095, (732) 636-4040
Woodbury: Kings Hwy., P.O. Box 363, 08096, (856) 845-4056
Wyckoff: P.O. Box 2, 07481, (201) 891-3616

Associations of New Jersey Business Owners

NATIONAL ALLIANCE OF HOMEBASED BUSINESSES (NAHB)
41 Wittmer Court, Princeton, New Jersey 08540
(609) 921-0308

NATIONAL ASSOCIATION OF WOMEN BUSINESS OWNERS (NAWBO)
1-800-55-NAWBO, www.nawbo.org
Central Jersey Chapter, www.nawbocentraljersey.org, (800)644-0709
North Central Jersey Chapter, www.nawboncj.org, (973)786-7095
South Jersey Chapter, www.nawbosouthjersey.org, (609)923-5889

NJ ASSOCIATION OF WOMEN BUSINESS OWNERS, INC. (NJAWBO)
127 US Hwy 206 Suite 28, Hamilton, New Jersey 08610
(609) 581-2121, www.njawbo.org

Helpful Links for Starting a Business in New Jersey

Small Business Administration   http://www.sba.gov/
Small Business Development Centers   http://www.njsbdc.com
SBA Frequently Requested Info.   http://www.sba.gov/map.html
SCORE   http://www.score.org/
State of New Jersey Division of Taxation

http://www.state.nj.us/treasury/taxation/index.html

Internal Revenue Service   http://www.irs.gov

Entrepreneurs (beginning business owners)

http://www.entrepreneur.com

NJ Chambers of Commerce and Business Associations

www.njchamber.com/Local-Chambers/chambers.htm

How to Start a Business in New Jersey   www.njbizbook.com

11
SELECTING AN ACCOUNTANT

Many people have approached me and asked the question — "How do you select an accountant?" Then when you do pick one, how do you know if he/she is really doing for you what you need? Here is an approach to help start your search for an accountant:

1. **Seek out someone who owns a business similar to yours.**
2. **Be sure that the size of the establishment and annual sales are on a par with your new business expectations.**
3. **Ask the owner to give you the name of his accountant.**
4. **Give the accountant a call, explain your situation and request an appointment.**

I have discovered that many new business owners decide to start their own venture without the advice or assistance of a professional. Some business owners will invest thousands of dollars, incorporate and sign long-term contracts without having contacted an accountant or attorney.

You should be sure to enlist the help of a professional accountant prior to starting your new business. The beginning fees will not be significant, but the advice you obtain will be immeasurable. This professional will help you select the proper type of enterprise, set up your books, apply for identification numbers, and prepare your tax forms.

Another source might be an accounting or business management instructor at a college. More than likely these individuals will have part-time accounting practices with a number of smaller clients. Approach any one of the instructors and inquire of their expertise in the area of your new venture. Ask if they have other clients in the same business. Then inquire if you can spend some time with them to discuss your new business.

There are also many seminars given during the year that are sponsored by the S.B.A., S.C.O.R.E., Chambers of Commerce, Small Business Development Center, Community Colleges, and the New

Jersey Office of Small Business. I suggest that you attend a few of these meetings for the information and literature that is distributed. Almost always there is an accountant present, giving a talk on the successful operation of a small business. This individual is one that you might want to seek out for professional advice in running your new business. Approach him/her to see if they could spend some time with you to review your business proposal.

More than likely the accountants will charge you some minimal fee for the time spent in their office. Don't waste their time, get to the point and present your case.

During the interview with the prospective accountant, pose the following questions, preferably in this order:

1. **Have you ever taken care of my type of business?**
2. **How often will you come to work on my account?**
3. **What will you do for me?**
4. **How often will you bill me?**
5. **How much will you charge for the work to be performed?**

Presently, the fee for most accountants who charge by the hour is $125 to $200 per hour. The average is about $150 per hour.

Here is what your accountant should do for you.

Always should be able to:

— **Prepare corporate or partnership tax forms**
— **Handle all I.R.S. audits**
— **Handle all New Jersey audits**
— **Prepare financial statements**
— **Prepare your personal tax form 1040**
— **Go to your bank with you when needed for a loan**

If not completed by you or your bookkeeper, your accountant should be able to:

— **Prepare Federal and State Payroll reports**
— **Prepare New Jersey business personal property tax forms**
— **Prepare New Jersey sales tax forms**
— **Prepare New Jersey gross income tax monthly forms**

- **Prepare monthly depository cards — FICA, Federal Withholding Tax**
- **Do checkbook bank reconciliation**
- **Write up a cash receipts and disbursements journal**
- **Set up and post to a general ledger**

Remember, no matter who you select as an accountant, be sure you are comfortable with this person. Don't pick someone just because your relative used them and their prices are low. They must instill some professional confidence in you and respect you as a client. Their advice is invaluable so make use of it, ask questions, and make sure you get what you pay for.

12
CONCLUSION

Now that you have read this manual, you should feel more confident to take that big step into the world of business ownership.

Being your own boss is great . . . when it works. Be sure to ask questions and seek professional assistance as soon as you feel the need for help.

The proper use of accounting and legal advice throughout your business career will hopefully prevent those major catastrophes that befall many new owners.

This manual has provided you with an introduction into the business environment. Take the time to acquire as much knowledge about your new business as possible. Subscribe to business magazines and read some of the small business texts that are available in your local library.

13
SUGGESTED READING FOR THE SMALL BUSINESS OWNER

GENERAL

Franchise Opportunities Handbook — For sale by Superintendent of Documents — U.S. Government Printing Office, Washington, D.C. 20402. Contains 340 pages of current franchises available; investment requirements and description of operation. Approximate cost $30.00.

S.B.A. Pamphlet 115A provides a list of over 100 publications available from the S.B.A., P.O. Box 15434, Fort Worth, Texas, 76119. Pamphlet 115B lists the For-Sale Publications.

Mind Your Own Business At Home (for home-based business), P.O. Box 14850, Chicago, Illinois 60614.

MAGAZINES AVAILABLE FOR THE BUSINESS OWNER

In Business — Box 323, Emmons, Pa. 18049, nine issues

Money by Time, Inc. — 3435 Wilshire Blvd., Los Angeles, California 90010

Venture — 35 West 45th Street, New York, New York 10036

Entrepreneur — 2311 Pontius Avenue, Los Angeles, California 90064

PAPERBACK AND HARDCOVER BOOKS

How to Pick the Right Small Business Opportunity, Albert, Kenneth, McGraw Hill

Starting and Succeeding in Your Own Small Business. Allen, Louis, Grosset and Dunlap

How to Organize and Operate a Small Business, Baumback, Clifford, Prentice Hall

Scratching Your Entrepreneurial Itch: A Guide to Business Venturing, Channing, Peter C., Hawthorn Books

The #1 Home Business Book, Delany, George, Liberty Publishing Co.

Four Hundred Two Things You Must Know Before Starting a New Business, Fox, Philip, Prentice Hall

Where Have All the Woolly Mammoths Gone — A Small Business Survival Manual, Frost, Ted S., CPA, Parker Publishing Company, Inc.

How to Start Your Own Craft Business, Genfran, Herb, Watson Guptill Publications

Word Processing Profits at Home, Glenn, Peggy, Aames-Allen Publishing Co.

Mail Order Magic, Holtz, Herman, McGraw Hill

Profit From Your Money Making Ideas, Holtz, Herman, Amacom

Woman's Guide to Starting a Business, Jessup, Claudia, HR & W Management

50 Big Money Businesses You Can Start and Run with $250 to $5,000, Kahm, H.S., Colphen Books

The Student Entrepreneur's Guide, Kingstone, Brett, Ten Sped Press

How to Run a Small Business, J.K. Lasser, Tax Institute, McGraw Hill

New Businesses Women Can Start and Successfully Operate, Leslie, Mary, Farnsworth Publishing Co.

Starting Your Own Secretarial Business, Lonngren, Betty, Contemporary Books, Inc.

Franchising: How To Select a Business, Metz, Robert, Hawthron Books

Financing the Growing Business, Martin, Thomas, Holt, Rinehard and Winston

How to Win S.B.A. Loans, Novete, J.S., Citizens Law Library

How To Start Your Own Small Business, Putt, William, Drake

How to Get Rich in Mail Order, Powers, Melan, Wilshire Book Co.

How to Earn Over $50,000 a Year at Home, Ramsey, Don, Parker Publishing Company

92

184 Businesses Anyone Can Start and Make a Lot of Money, Revel, Chase, Bantam Books

One Hundred Thirty Two Ways to Earn a Living Without Working for Someone Else, Rosenthal, Ed. St. Martin's Press

Small Business Guide to Borrowing Money, Rubin, Richard, McGraw Hill

How to Make Money at Home, Shelbor, Sharon, Simon and Schuster, Publisher

The following is a series of paperback books published by the Wiley Press, 605 Third Avenue, New York, N.Y. 10158. This small business series is advertised by the publisher as practical how-to-do-it guides for the small business owner.

How To Run A Successful Specialty Food Store, by Douglass L. Brownstone

Successful Selling Skills for Small Business, by David M. Brownstone

How To Run A Successful Florist & Plant Store, by Bram Cavin

Efficient Accounting and Record-Keeping, by Dennis M. Doyle

How To Open and Run a Money-Making Travel Agency, by Pamela Fremont

How To Set Up and Run A Typing Service, by Donna Goodrich

How To Start, Run and Stay in Business, by Gregory F. Kishel & Patricia Gunter Kishel

Financing Your Small Business, by Egon W. Loffel

From Rags to Riches — Success in Apparel Retailing by Marvin E. Segal

How To Advertise and Promote Your Small Business, by Gonnie McClung Siegel

Franchising, by William L. Siegel

How To Run A Successful Restaurant, by William L. Siegel

People Management for Small Business, by William L. Siegel